D0539450

WORLD FAMOUS
UFOs

WORLD FAMOUS
UFOs

Colin Wilson

‖ ·PARRAGON· ‖

This edition published and distributed by Parragon,
produced by Magpie Books,
an imprint of Robinson Publishing, London

Parragon
Unit 13–17,
Avonbridge Trading Estate,
Atlantic Road,
Avonmouth,
Bristol,
BS11 9QD

Copyright © Robinson Publishing Ltd

All rights reserved. No part of this publication may be
reproduced, stored in a retrieval system, or transmitted, in
any form or by any means, electronic, mechanical,
photocopying, recording, or otherwise, without the prior
permission of Robinson Publishing

ISBN 0 75251 785 6

British Library Cataloguing-in-Publication Data
A catalogue record for this book is available
from the British Library

10 9 8 7 6 5 4 3 2 1

CONTENTS

Chapter one: **The Coming of the Saucers**   1
Earlier UFO Sightings   4
The UFO Craze   9
European Sighting   15

Chapter two: **Mysteries and Mystifications**   23

Chapter three: **Who Are They?**   47
The Dogon   54
Jung on Flying Saucers   58
Are They Fairies?   61
John Keel on UFOs   68

Chapter four: **Cover-Up?**   75
Project Blue Book   75

Chapter five: **The Psychic Solution?**   93
The Loch Ness Ghost?   93
Puharich and Geller   101

Chapter six: **Aliens Among Us?**   115
Conclusions   157

Chapter One

THE COMING OF THE SAUCERS

'**F** lying saucers' are undoubtedly the major unsolved mystery of the second half of the twentieth century – by comparison, the Loch Ness Monster, the Abominable Snowman, even the Burmuda Triangle seem local and altogether less baffling.

There have been many explanations, from Jung's belief that they were 'all in the mind' to the suggestion that they might be some kind of ghost or supernatural occurrence. Those who believe in their physical reality divide fairly equally into two groups: those who believe that there are hostile aliens, whose intentions towards the human race are wholly sinister, to those who prefer to accept that their intention is basically benevolent, and that their purpose is to teach the human race to avoid disaster. In fact, even Jung ended his life by accepting that Unidentified Flying Objects are real and objective, although he's not on record as taking any view of their purpose. In late June, 1947, a C46 Transport aircraft disappeared in the area of Mount Rainier, in Washington State, with thirty-two men on board. A five thousand dollar reward was offered for anyone who could locate the aircraft. Kenneth Arnold, an Idaho businessman who was also an experienced pilot, decided to try for the prize, and took off in his small propeller-driven monoplane on the morning of 24 June, 1947 from the airfield at Chehalis to fly across the Cascade Mountains to Yakima, Washington State.

Later that day, he was to describe how, flying at an altitude of about 9200 feet above the town of Mineral, he was beginning to make a 180 degrees turn when 'a tremendously bright flash lit up the surface of my aircraft.' A moment later, he saw another flash and saw 'far to my left and to the north, a formation of nine very bright objects coming from the vicinity of Mount Baker, flying very close to the mountaintops and travelling at a tremendous speed.' Since they were travelling at almost 90 degrees to Arnold's flight path, he was able to calculate this speed at 1700 m.p.h. Moreover, the craft were not flying in the straight trajectory of a normal aircraft, but bobbing up and down 'like speed boats on rough water.' 'They fluttered and sailed, tipping their wings alternately and emitting very bright blue-white flashes from their surfaces.'

Arnold was so intrigued that he decided to land at Yakima and report the sighting. He landed at about four in the afternoon and told his story to a manager and discussed it with other pilots, before taking off again for Pendleton, Oregon. By the time he arrived there, he found that the news had preceded him, and that among the crowd waiting to receive him was a reporter named Bill Becquette, from the *East Oregonian* newspaper. It was to him that Arnold used the classic phrase that would echo throughout the rest of the century: that the objects moved 'like a saucer would if you skipped it across water.' So began the mystery of the 'flying saucers'.

Yet if we look again at the original description of the craft, it is notable that Arnold said 'tipping their *wings* alternately' which certainly sounds as if he mistook them for normal aeroplanes.

Arnold's first conclusion is that they were some secret weapon of the United States Air Force, perhaps some type of robot craft like the German 'flying bombs' of the end of the Second World War.

As a result of Becquette's story — which was carried by the Associated Press wire service, Arnold suddenly found himself famous. For three days, he talked endlessly to reporters. It was only when he was back at home in Boise, Idaho, that he was told by the aviation editor of a local newspaper that what he had seen was pretty definitely nothing to do with the Air Force or the United States Government. Later on, Arnold was to come to the odd conclusion that what he had seen was some strange unknown species of animal that inhabit the upper layers of the earth's atmosphere — a theory reminiscent of Conan Doyle's story 'The Horror of the Heights'.

For some reason, the world was ready for strange stories about Unidentified Flying Objects. The end of the war had seen London attacked by Hitler's V-2 rockets, and after the war, many of the German scientists who worked on the rockets — notably Werner von Braun — were persuaded to go to America to work on the effort to put a man on the moon. Popular magazines were full of articles about space flight, and the possibility of life on other planets. So all over the world, people were ready to take this first sighting of 'Flying Saucers' seriously.

What happened next is almost as interesting as Arnold's original sighting. The news literally unleashed a flood of UFO sightings. The first came three days later, when a Washington housewife saw discs 'like silver plates' flying over the Cascade Mountains, near where Arnold had spotted them. The following day, 28 June, saw three more sightings, one by a pilot over Lake Meade, Nevada, one over Maxwell Air Force Base in Montgomery, Alabama and one at Rockfield, Wisconcin, when a farmer saw some blue, soundless discs flying over his farm. The next few weeks saw dozens more, including no less than eighty-eight sightings on Independence Day, 4 July, reported by four hundred people in twenty-four states. On 7 July, the first British sighting occurred when a married couple saw 'something like a moon, only bigger' fly over the cliffs at Brighton. On the same day, astronomers at Del Salto Observatory, Chile, saw a disc trailing white gases and moving across the horizon at what they estimated at 3000 m.p.h. On the same day, more UFOs were reported in Italy, Japan and Holland.

Mass hysteria? Some of it certainly was. Yet at least one of the sightings – the one over Maxwell Air Force Base – included a detail that certainly adds to its authenticity. The bright light that zig-zagged at high speed made a sharp right angle turn before disappearing.

In fact, this is a highly characteristic observation, of the kind that no-one would have thought of inventing at the time. But it has been reported again and again in subsequent cases.

Earlier UFO Sightings

Between 1925 and 1927, the Russian painter Nicholas Roerich, known in the west mainly for his designs for the Diaghilev Ballet, including Stravinsky's *Rite of Spring* – was travelling from Mongolia to India across the Himalayas. In his book *Altai-Himalaya* (1930) Roerich describes how, on August 5th, 1926, the whole party observed a big, shiny disc moving at great speed across the sky and then quite abruptly changing direction above their camp. Roerich's description attracted no attention until after the 'flying saucer craze' began in 1947. But then, ufologists (a term coined many years later) began to draw attention to the accounts of shining objects in the sky which had been described for centuries.

At the present writing, priority must be given to an account contained in Egyptian papyrus from the reign of the pharoah Thutmose III, who came to the throne around the year 1500 BC. A papyrus in the Vatican Library describes how 'in the year 22, of the 3rd month of the winter, 6th hour of the day . . . the scribes of the House of Life found there was a circle of fire coming in the sky . . . it had no head, the breath of its mouth had a foul odour. Its body was one rod (5 metres) long and one rod wide.' Here the description of its foul breath suggests that it came close enough to leave behind some kind of smell, which suggests a meteorite. This impression seems to be supported by the fact that on the following days 'these things became more numerous in the sky than ever.'

Students of the Bible came up with some rather dubious examples. The description of the Pillar of Fire that guided the Israelites, led by Moses, out of Egypt is quite clearly not a flying saucer. Neither is the Chariot of Fire in which the prophet Elijah was carried up into heaven, as described in the second *Book of Kings*. And visions of the prophet Ezekiel – four of them – of whirlwinds and clouds of fire must also be dismissed on the grounds that the majority of UFO sightings involve discs of light, not clouds of fire. The same, on the whole, applies to most of the examples deployed by Josef F. Blumrich (an employee of NASA) in *The Spaceships of Ezekiel*.

According to the chroniclers of Alexander the Great, he had two UFO experiences. In 329 BC, when Alexander was invading India, two 'shining silver shields' dived out of the sky and harassed his soldiers, whose elephants and horses scattered in all directions. But seven years later, five UFOs – all shining shields – in V formation helped him to gain entrance to a city he was besieging when the leading UFO fired a beam of light which knocked a hole through the city wall.

In his *Complete Catalogue of UFO Sightings*, Peter Brooke-smith lists no less than six sightings in Ancient Rome, but most of these 'globes of fire' in the sky sound more like meteorites than UFOs. The same applies to the eighteen sightings from medieval Europe that he lists: the only one that sounds remotely like a modern sighting is the 'flat, round, shining silvery object' that William of Newburgh describes in his *Chronicle* flying over Byland Abbey in Yorkshire in 1290 AD. The rest — fiery dragons, burning crosses and blood red balls — may have been genuine 'unidentified flying objects' but do not sound remotely like Flying Saucers.

A notable exception among early reports dates from the year 1878, when, according to the *Denison Daily News* of Texas, USA, it described how 'Mr John Martin, a farmer . . . had his attention directed to a dark object high in the northern sky. The peculiar shape and velocity with which the object seemed to approach, riveted his attention, and he strained his eyes . . . when first noticed it appeared to be about the size of an orange, after which it continued to grow in size. After gazing at it for some time Mr Martin became blind from looking and left off viewing to rest his eyes. On resuming his view, the object was almost overhead and had increased considerably in size and appeared to be going through space at a wonderful speed. When directly over him, the object was the size of a large saucer and . . . at a great height.'

Here the word 'saucer' is used for the first time, and since he'd hurt his eyes, we can also assume that — in spite of its first dark appearance — it shone in a manner typical of modern UFOs.

One of the first writers to make a habit of noting down reports of 'unknown objects seen in the skies' was Charles Fort. Born in Albany, N.Y. in 1874, he made a poor living as a journalist for most of his life. In revolt against his bad tempered father, he spent his life finding reasons for undermining authority.

In 1916, when he was forty-two, a small legacy enabled him to spend his days in the New York Public Library, searching periodicals for accounts of strange and unexplained events. His four books — beginning with *The Book of the Damned* (1919) should have made him famous and rich, since his fellow Americans have an unquenchable appetite for strange stories and extraordinary theories. Unfortunately, Fort was short on theory — his method was simply to take any odd events he could find and throw them higgledy-piggledy into books that had no particular direction or argument. Fort simply had no gift of story telling, with the consequence that, when he died in 1932, he was virtually as unknown as when he started.

But his miscellaneous collections of 'damned' (by damned he meant excluded by science) facts are like old attics full of rubbish through which other collectors can rummage for hours — provided they can stand the dust.

Among Fort's typical observations are the following: 'Maunder was at the Royal Observatory, Greenwich, November 17, 1882, at night . . . In the midst of the Aurora a great circular disc of greenish light appeared and moved smoothly across the sky . . . the thing passed above the moon, and was, by other observers, described as "cigar-shaped", "like a torpedo", "a spindle", "a shuttle." '

This seems to be the first recording of the typical 'cigar-shaped' UFO that has been reported so frequently.

Here is another: 'I was standing on the corner of Church and College Street . . . when, without the slightest indication or warning, we were startled by what sounded like a most unusual and terrific explosion . . . raising my eyes, and looking eastward along College, I observed a torpedo-shaped body, some 300 feet away, stationary in appearance, and suspended in the air, about 50 feet above the tops of the buildings . . . This object

Flying saucer photographed in Almagordo, New Mexico

soon began to move, rather slowly, and disappeared over Dolan Brothers' store, southward. As it moved, the covering seemed to be rupturing in places, and through these the intensely red flames issued.'

Fort's biographer Damon Knight comments: 'The reports of unknown flying objects collected by Fort bear little resemblance, as a rule, to the "flying saucer" stereotype. Some were simply moving lights in the sky, some torpedo-shaped, some triangular. Others were like nothing on Earth, but showed definite evidence of structure. There was a "thing" seen by the crew of the barque *Lady of the Lake* on March 22, 1870.'

The UFO Craze

During the next ten years there were thousands of sightings — so many that it would be impossible even to mention most of them. But one of the most controversial — the so-called 'Roswell incident' — is still hotly debated.

From an early stage, the US government and Air Force had shown a tendency to denounce UFO sightings as hallucinations, or to insist that the observers had seen something else — the planet Venus, a weather balloon, an ordinary aeroplane seen at an angle where the wings were not visible. This in turn gave plausibility to rumours of a cover-up, the notion that the government really knew all about visitors from outer space, but were deliberately keeping it secret for sinister reasons of their own.

Roswell is a town in Lincoln County, New Mexico. On 2 July, 1947, a hardware dealer named Dan Wilmot was sitting at dusk with his wife on the front porch of their house when they were startled by a shining object 'like two inverted saucers faced mouth to mouth' flashing across the sky from the south east. A few minutes later, above the Foster ranch 75 miles away, Mac Brazel heard a loud explosion which might have been the sound of thunder. The next morning he found wreckage trailing across his land for 400 yards. He described it as 'metallic foil-like substance' like some kind of thin metal sheet. It was so springy that Brazel was unable to give it a permanent bend or crease – even a blow torch and a sledge hammer failed to make any permanent impression on it.

There had been a number of UFO sightings in the area, and Brazel reported the wreckage to the American army at Roswell. An Intelligence Officer returned with him to look at the metal, and the following day, troops arrived and removed it all – in the meantime keeping sightseers away.

Six days later, on 8 July 1947, a civil engineer named Grady L. Barnett who came from nearby Socorro, reported seeing an object that he thought was a crashed aircraft. He later claimed that what he found was 'some sort of metallic, disc-shaped object' about 30 feet in diameter, which had been torn open by its impact. Inside, he claimed, he found three small, hairless bodies – humanoid creatures with large heads and wearing grey one-piece suits. A number of archaeology students joined him there. At this point, a US army jeep arrived, and declared the area off limits, sending them all away. They were also warned not to speak about what they had seen. But that day, the *Roswell Daily Record* reported that a flying disc had been found and recovered from a ranch 75 miles away – the report was authorised by the base commander at Roswell. The army acted swiftly to defuse the intense excitement caused by the announcement. The same day, they called two press conferences and explained that the debris found by Brazell was the remains of a weather balloon. The intelligence officer who had first seen it — Major Jesse Marcel — was photographed with some of this material. In the photograph the material is quite obviously the torn skin of a weather balloon, and there is certainly no question of it being a thin metal sheet that could not be permanently bent or folded.

As far as the army was concerned, that was the end of the Roswell Incident.

UFO enthusiasts naturally took a different view. And a television programme shown in 1995 left no doubt whatsoever that they were correct. The programme featured many witnesses who had been present at the time, including Major Marcel himself, who admitted the cover-up. The local radio reporter told how a General from the Pantagon had threatened to close the station down the same day if they broadcast any more about it. One woman was threatened with death if she spoke of the strange metallic material that she had seen and touched. A master sergeant described a post mortem held on the three child-sized aliens in the craft, and there is even film footage that claims to show this post mortem. All of which leaves us with the question: *why* did the Air Force engage in such a cover-up? Were they afraid that the 'landing' might cause mass panic? That hardly seems plausible. Whatever the answer, the Roswell Incident leaves no doubt whatever that — in this case at least — the armed forces engaged in deliberate deception.

But the incident that caused the widest publicity — and convinced the general public that UFOs really existed — was the death of US pilot Thomas Mantell while apparently chasing a flying saucer. On the 7 January, 1948, the control tower at Godman Field near Fort Knox, Kentucky, was notified that a number of local residents had reported a UFO sighting. In fact, it was seen near the base that afternoon. Two hours later, at about 3 o'clock, five P-51 Fighters, led by Captain Thomas Mantell, took off to

Sceptics who dismissed the UFO phenomenon as some kind of mass hysteria often cited the interesting case of the great Martian panic of 1938. At eight o'clock on the evening of October 30, 1938, the announcer of the Columbia Broadcasting System in New York told listeners that Orson Welles was about to present his own version of *The War of the Worlds* by H.G. Wells.

In fact, Welles had listened to the original recording of the show, and decided it was too dull. He thought it might be livened up by presenting it as if it was a genuine news broadcast.

The result was that the programme started with some dance music, which was interrupted by an announcer saying that an astronomical observatory had noticed a series of gas explosions on the planet Mars. It was then announced that a meteorite had fallen at Grovers Mill in New Jersey, killing several people. After this there was more music, then a series of interruptions which culminated in the announcer declaring: 'I have a grave announcement to make. Incredible as it seems, the strange beings who landed in New Jersey tonight are the vanguard of an army from the planet Mars!' After this, a statement from someone who claimed to be the Secretary of the Interior in Washington declared that Martians had landed all over the country and were slaughtering Americans with death rays. New York itself was surrounded by Martians.

Twenty minutes after the programme began, cars full of families were speeding at seventy and eighty miles an hour out of New York and Philadelphia. All over the country, police stations were besieged with enquiries, and as the panic grew, rumour had it that the invaders were actually Germans, Japanese or Chinese. Many people who had tuned in to the programme halfway through were convinced that American civilisation was on the brink of destruction. All over the country, panic-stricken people rushed out of their houses like stampeding cattle.

Welles knew nothing of this, although at half past eight, he was told that a dozen policemen wanted to see him. Since he was tied up in the studio, the broadcast went on.

As the programmed finished the announcer screaming from the top of the CBS building that Time Square and Fifth Avenue were overrun with the Martian invaders wielding death rays, a furious phone-call from the Mayor of a mid-western city declared that women and children were huddled in the churches, looters were smashing shop windows, and if all this was a joke he personally was coming to New York to punch Orson Welles on the nose.

In New Jersey, the National Guard was mobilised, and in San Francisco a man phoned the police asking where he could volunteer to fight the Martians.

When CBS realised what a panic the broadcast had caused, they made announcements every ten minutes telling the listeners that it was just a play.

The 'invasion from Mars' had the effect of making Orson Welles famous, and obtaining a number of enthusiastic sponsors for his drama series, which had so far been unsponsored.

After Doctor Edward Condon had announced that flying saucers definitely did not exist, the *Denver Post* published a cartoon showing Condon being dragged off towards a flying saucer by two little green men with radio aerials sticking out of their heads, while a number of alarmed men standing in the doorway of the University of Colorado Department for National UFO Study shouted after him: 'Stay calm, Doctor Condon – just tell them you don't believe in them.'

investigate. Unfortunately, the planes did not possess oxygen cylinders, and four of them dropped out as they passed the official limit of 14,000 feet for their type of aircraft. Mantell who had told the control tower that he was chasing a UFO that was 'metallic and tremendous in size, and appears to be moving about half my speed' continued to chase it. He was last seen at 3.15, continuing to climb. This was the last that was heard from him. Nearly two hours later, at 5 o'clock, the wreckage of his aircraft was found near Franklin, Kentucky. The time of the impact was recorded by his watch, which had stopped at 3.18.

It seemed obvious that Mantell had simply blacked out as he had run out of oxygen – he was well above 22,000 feet when he ceased to call the tower. But rumours soon spread that he had been shot down by a UFO. The Air Force made things worse by explaining that the UFO reported near the base had actually been the planet Venus, and then, realising that this was implausible during the day, that it was a weather balloon.

On the whole, this explanation seems plausible. The fact that the object was moving at only half the speed of Mantell's aircraft and that those who saw it described it as white, and 'umbrella-shaped' makes it sound more like a weather balloon than the usual fast-moving UFO.

European Sighting

'On January 7th, 1954, at 4.26 a.m., M. Brevart, a baker at Arras, was working in his bakehouse when he thought he would step outside for a breath of fresh air. Scarcely had he done so than a strange glow in the sky made him look upwards. At a point just above the Place de la Vacquerie behind the town hall, a luminous disc as big as the full moon, but much brighter, was hanging motionless. M. Brevart, startled and incredulous, rubbed his eyes, but the object was undoubtedly there and apparently not very far above the town. It remained in this position for several seconds, and then suddenly started a rocking movement, discharged a dazzling flash of light which illuminated the whole of the Place, described a semi-circle and vanished at an immense speed in the direction of St Pol-sur-Ternoize, nearer the coast, filling the sky with an enormous orange-coloured radiance.

'Almost at the same moment, at 7.27, a railway man who was on duty at Orchies, about 25 miles north-east of Arras as the crow flies, saw a shining disc vanishing towards the south-west. It was moving horizontally at an

UFOs seen in Brazil, 1969

enormous speed, with the vivid orange-coloured light trailing behind it.

'A few seconds later the whole of the Seine-Inférieure department from Fécamp in the west to Dieppe in the north, Mailleraye in the south to Gournay in the east, was lit up by what seemed to be a huge fire in the sky. For half a minute the light was so bright that the railwaymen at Serqueux were able to see the registration numbers of the carriages. A few minutes later Dieppe was suddenly shaken by a tremendous explosion which smashed a large number of windows and woke up most of the people in the town.

'That evening a spokesman of the Astrophysical Institute of Paris made the following statement: "It is very probable that the phenomenon seen this morning in the Dieppe area was a meteorite".'

The Institute failed to explain why the meteorite was hanging suspended above the Town Hall.

This incident is recorded by the first of the major French Flying Saucer experts, Aimé Michel, in a book called *The Truth About Flying Saucers* (1956). The distinguished man of letters Jean Cocteau provided an introduction; like Charles Fort, he took the opportunity to thumb his nose at authority. 'We must hope that the new satellites observed 600 kilometres from our globe in the last few months are not the checkpoints and artificial garages of these swift and silent vehicles. We must also hope that the whole thing remains a theory and will not humble the pride which blinds mankind and leaves it to think that what it does not know is impossible.'

Michel's book is an excellent history of UFO sightings until that time – beginning with Kenneth Arnold, but also including a number of earlier ones. The most interesting part of his book is the second half, where he writes at length of all the important sightings so far over Europe. Many of these were seen in the clear skies of Africa. A report from Bocaranga on 22 November, 1952, is typical of them. Father Carlos Maria had hitched a lift with a businessman from Bouar to go and see his dentist. Father Carlos describes how in a tree-lined road at dusk, 'we suddenly saw a large disc which seemed to be about to traverse the sky ahead and was rather low down.' This disappeared, but sometime afterwards, they were obliged to stop to refuel. At this point, eight of them were able to see 'four discs hanging in the sky to the left of the road. We could see them quite clearly, although it was impossible to judge their distance. There were two above and two below, and they were not in contact. When they came to a standstill they were pale silver in colour, like the moon.

'I had several opportunities of seeing them in motion and had a strong idea that the lower pair only were revolving. Just before moving, they blazed up as bright as the sun. Then they seemed to arrange themselves in a group which proceeded to describe circles before returning to their starting point. When they stopped, the bright blaze died down to the original dull silver . . . We were watching them from 10 to 10.20 p.m. After their final circling movement they remained motionless for several minutes. Then they departed and disappeared in the opposite direction to ours, still keeping to the left of the road. Such at least was my impression, but I do not rule out the possibility that they might never have moved and that I might have been deceived by a gradual diminution of luminosity until they were lost in the darkness of the night.'

Michel goes on to consider Father Carlos Maria's story at considerable length, carefully examining every detail. Then, in the logical manner of the French, he does his best to explain it with a theory. This theory is not his own, but is that of one 'Lieutenant Plantier', 'one of the most brilliant brains in the new French Air Force.' Bored to death in a minor post, Lieutenant Plantier devoted his mind to the problem of inventing a machine capable of escaping the gravitational pull of the earth. Jet propelled rockets, he thought, were crude and wasteful. Surely it ought to be possible to make use of the energy of cosmic rays, the radiation that reaches earth from some unknown point in space, which seems to consist largely of highly charged protons moving at a very high speed. These, says Lieutenant Plantier, contain energy amounting to about a hundred thousand times the energy to split an atomic nucleus.

Plantier's idea was that it ought to be possible to transform the energy of cosmic rays into energies of a lower kind — 'like the blow of the hammer upon the anvil, which transforms kinetic energy into calorific energy.'

Plantier's next question was: suppose you were asked to invent a machine that would transform cosmic rays into 'usable energy', where would you start? He mentions a device called the 'photometric propeller' which revolves because one side of its blades is painted black, and black absorbs light while the other, painted white, does not. 'Light sails' on spacecraft make use of the same principle, and are driven by a hail of photons from the sun.

If a machine could be created which absorbed this cosmic energy and could make use of it, it would be driven along on exactly the same principle as a photometric propeller. 'There would be thus a kind of continuous jet, pulsating right through the machine. Released by the machine, it would follow it on it's journey, propel it, and hold it up when it stopped, very like the jets of water on which ping-pong balls are poised in shooting galleries at fairs.' Plantier then went on to say 'to achieve its full efficiency, the machine must be in the form of a disc which is perfectly symmetrical in relation to its axis.' Moreover: 'the machine could travel at the most terrifying speeds without producing a sound, and break through the sound barrier without producing the transonic bang.' This is because the force field of the machine would drag the surrounding air along with it. Each successive layer of air would drag the next layer along with it at a slightly slower speed, and so on. This would mean that 'the machine could move through the atmosphere at enormous speeds without experiencing any increase of temperature.' And since the machine contains a field of force which includes the passengers, the passengers would not notice the tremendous acceleration, even if it went at thousands of miles an hour.

Michel goes on: 'Lieutenant Plantier had reached this point in his reasoning when a crazy notion entered his head, a notion which I am sure has entered the reader's — his impossible contrivance, a brain child born of the boredom of an outlandish military station, *already existed*. He had seen it. It was the flying saucer.'

According to Plantier, his machine would have to oscillate for a fraction of a second and then tilt at 'a very marked angle' in order to take off. This, he says, has been observed in the case of flying saucers. He worked out that this tilting of the machine would be accomplished by a screen inside it, capable of changing position. The movements of this screen would be visible outside the machine in the form of a patch of light below it — again, something that many observers of flying saucers have noticed. Above the machine, Plantier calculated, there would probably be a patch of cloud, even in a completely blue sky, because the field of force would cause an upward rush of air above the machine which would produce condensation. Plantier describes a UFO sighting by an Air Force pilot called René Sacle on December 29, 1952 at Courcon-d'Aunis, Charente-Maritime, who saw, to his amazement, a lonely little cumulonimbus rise vertically in the clear blue sky and then cast off something vague and shapeless which rapidly disappeared, leaving a white trail behind it.

According to Aimé Michel, Plantier has solved the basic riddle of the flying saucers: how they work. They are machines that somehow make use of the energy of cosmic rays.

Chapter Two

MYSTERIES AND MYSTIFICATIONS

O ne of the earliest books on Flying Saucers, *The Case For the UFO*, appeared in 1955. The author was Doctor Morris K. Jessup, who taught astronomy and mathematics at the University of Michigan, and his astronomical researches led to the discovery of thousands of binary stars. Jessup shared Charles Fort's ability to cast his net wide, and his book includes interesting historical material on past sightings of UFOs, and accounts of strange disappearances that he thinks may be attributable to UFOs. One of these, cited from the writer R. Dewitt Miller, author of *Forgotten Mysteries*, has achieved a kind of classic status.

'On September 23, 1880, David Lang, a farmer and prominent landowner living near Gallatin, Tennessee, returned home from a business trip. After greeting his family, he started across an 80 acre field to inspect his blooded horses.

'While he was walking across the field, his wife and two children saw a buggy approach along the road, and Lang stopped. In the buggy were Judge Peck, a local attorney, and a friend. When he saw Lang crossing the field, Peck stopped in his buggy and signalled the farmer to return to his house.

'There, in full view of five persons – Lang's wife and two children, Peck and his friend – Lang vanished in a field which was devoid of trees, boulders, or any sort of cover; a field covered with grass and without caves, bogs, abandoned wells, or other chasms. In fact, a later geological survey showed this entire field was underlayed at a depth of a few feet with a solid stratum of limestone.

'The press of Tennessee was filled for months with stories about the "Lang disappearance". There were searches — made immediately following Lang's vanishing and for months afterwards.

'Bloodhounds were used. Detectives were called in. The story reached Vienna, and a Doctor Hern stated that: "There are vortices (in the so-called physical world) through which a man might vanish." Ambrose Bierce wrote a fictionalised version of the incident. The bloodhounds, the detectives and the theorists produce nothing.

'The case has been the subject of endless speculation. But no-one has ever found a trace of David Lang. And there remains only the affidavit of Lang's daughter and the statements of the other witnesses that Lang simply vanished while crossing an open field.'

Jessup concludes this section: 'I submit that capture by a space contraption, for purposes beyond our ken, is the only truly satisfactory answer.'

Regrettably, Jessup was incorrect. When I asked a friend in Tennessee to investigate the case, I discovered that in fact, a hardware salesman called Joe McHatten, having spent a boring day in Gallatin confined to his room by snow, had whiled away the time by writing his wife a letter in which he had invented the whole story.

Soon after the publication of *The Case For the UFO*, Jessup received two letters from a man who signed himself Carlos Allende (or Carl Allen) who made an extraordinary claim: that in October 1943, the US Navy had tried inducing a tremendously powerful magnetic field on board a destroyer in Philadelphia. As a result, the ship became completely invisible while sailors on board became semi-transparent to one another's eyes. The ship itself vanished from its Philadelphia dock and reappeared at its other regular dock at Newport, Virginia. Half the crew, said Allende, became insane.

All this greatly excited Jessup, because he had already formulated a similar theory about how UFOs can appear and disappear. He connected it with Einstein's 'Unified Field Theory', which states, briefly, that 'our compartmentalised concept of time-space and matter-energy are not separate entities but are transmutable under the same conditions of electro-magnetic disturbance.'

When he had been corresponding with Allende for some time, Jessup received an unexpected request to come to Washington by the Office of Naval Research (ONR), and was shown a copy of his own book with notes in three different hand-writings. He thought he recognised one of these as that of Allende. Subsequently, the department of Naval Research had twenty-five copies of the book duplicated, and apparently sent to various offices in the department.

Three years later, in April 1959, Jessup was found dead in his parked station-wagon in Dade County Park, Miami, with a hose connecting the exhaust to the interior of the car. Jessup's friend Doctor Manson Valentine, told Charles Berlitz (who reports it in his book *The Burmuda Triangle*) that Jessup had been approached by the Navy to continue working on the Philadelphia Experiment or similar projects, but had declined. Valentine admits that 'some people' refused to believe that Jessup committed suicide, and that there were 'people or influences that wished to prevent' the spread of his theories.

And so, as early as the mid-1950s, the 'conspiracy theories' had begun; so had the rumours about aliens abducting human beings for their own mysterious purposes.

In fact, stories of contact with these alien beings had been circulating since soon after Kenneth Arnold's original sighting near Mount Rainier. Only a month later, on July

23, 1947, a group of survey workers at Bauru, in Brazil, saw a large metallic disc settle down on curved legs not far from them. All but one took to their heels. The man who remained, Jose Higgins, claims that he found himself face to face with three seven-foot-tall humanoids, all wearing transparent overalls, with metal boxes on their backs. He claims that they had large bald heads, big round eyes, no eyebrows, and long legs. After this, they dug some holes in the ground, and began throwing large boulders about. From the position of the holes in the ground, Higgins guessed that they were trying to indicate the position of planets with regard to the sun, and noticed that they pointed with particular insistence at the seventh of these holes. It was later speculated that they were trying to indicate that they came from the planet Uranus. After this, they re-entered their craft, which took off with a great whistling noise. The account appeared in two Brazilian newspapers.

In England in 1957, a Birmingham housewife claimed to have been visited by a spaceman in her own home. He did not arrive in a flying saucer, but simply materialised, accompanied by a whistling sound, in the living-room of 27 year old Mrs Cynthia Appleton. He was tall and fair and wore a tight-fitting plastic-like garment. He communicated, according to Mrs Appleton, by TELEPATHY, and produced tv-like pictures to illustrate his flying saucer and a larger master craft. He indicated to her that he came from a place of harmony and peace. At the end of all this, he simply dematerialised.

Three weeks later, on August 14, 1947, a professor named Johannis was walking in the mountains near Friuli, Italy, when he saw a large metallic disc, and two dwarf-like creatures, less than three feet tall, wearing translucent blue overalls with red collars and belts. Johannis claims that when he waved an alpine pick at them, one of them raised a hand to his belt, which emitted a puff of smoke, and caused the pick to fly out of the professor's hand. One of the 'spacemen' then took the pick, and they retreated into their craft, which shot into the air.

Three days later, in Death Valley, California, two prospectors witnessed what seemed to be the crash-landing of a Flying Saucer, and saw two small beings emerge from it. Chased by the prospectors they vanished amongst the sand dunes, and when the prospectors went back, the craft had disappeared.

But it was in 1953 that the most sensational account so far of 'alien contact' was published. It was a book called *Flying Saucers Have Landed*, by George Adamski and a journalist named Desmond Leslie.

Adamski, who was a counter assistant at a hamburger bar on the slopes of Mount Palomar — the home of the great observatory — and who awarded himself the honorary degree of 'professor', claimed to have been seeing UFOs since 1946 — that is, a year before Kenneth Arnold. He also claimed that on 5 March, 1951, he had photographed a giant cigar-shaped craft surrounded by smaller UFOs which emerged from it, and had taken another similar picture in the following year.

Adamski stated that, on 20 November, 1952, he had accompanied six friends into the California desert. These included another author called George H. Williamson, also a writer on Flying Saucers, who was to claim in one of his books that UFOs were stabled in a hangar under

The Pyramids at Giza, Egypt

the Great Pyramid, which was built by spacemen twenty-four thousand years ago.

According to Adamski, his hunch that they would be granted a 'sighting' was justified when, 'riding high, and without sound, there was a gigantic cigar-shaped silvery ship, without wings or appendages of any kind.' Adamski asked to be taken down the road, and his companions then returned to their original parking spot. When a number of aircrafts suddenly appeared and circled the cigar-shaped ship, it turned and vanished. But at this point, Adamski saw a flash in the sky and 'a beautiful craft appeared to be drifting through a saddle between two of the mountain peaks.' Adamski then saw a man beckoning to him from the opening of a ravine, and as he approached him, realised that he was looking at a visitor from another world.

The alien had 'wavy shoulder length sandy hair, and suntanned skin.' He had a high forehead, calm grey green eyes that slanted, high cheek bones, and 'a finely chiselled' nose. He was wearing a brown single-piece suit.

Communicating telepathically, the alien explained that he was from the planet Venus, and after a conversation, he was picked up by a flying saucer and flew away. Adamski's six companions, who then joined him, found a footprint in the sand.

The alien returned a month later, and this time Adamski was allowed to take photographs of the saucer, which he reproduced in his book.

This became an instant best-seller, and Adamski lost no time in following it up with a book called *Inside the Flying Saucers* (1955) in which he described how the aliens had taken him on a trip around the moon, and how he had seen rivers and lakes on its far side – the side which is permanently turned away from the earth.

Adamski's preposterous stories took in a surprising number of people. His co-author Desmond Leslie was later to admit that when he co-authored *Flying Saucers Have Landed*, he had never met him. 'My publisher and I both agreed that there was sufficient evidence in his testimony that he had contacted a flying saucer on the ground, to warrant publishing his narrative. Later events proved that we were justified . . .' And in a later book, *Flying Saucers Farewell* (1961) another flying saucer enthusiast, C.A. Honey, (who had known Kenneth Arnold) announced his total belief in Adamski — whom he claimed was 'as distinguished as a college professor' — and who claimed that the US State Department was trying to cover up its knowledge of the reality of flying saucers.

Adamski died in 1965 — at the age of 78 — and so succeeded in escaping the discrediting he deserved when the age of space flight revealed that the backside of the moon was as bleak as its front, and that the temperature on Venus was far too high to sustain life.

Adamski's success made more 'alien contacts' inevitable. In a book called *Aboard a Flying Saucer* (1953) Truman Bethurum described meeting little green men — or at least, olive men — who wore uniforms and came from a planet called Clarion which is permanently hidden behind the moon.

He also met an incredibly beautiful woman called Aura Rhanes who spent the night with him — disappointingly, only in conversation. Daniel Fry described meeting an alien in the desert in New Mexico whose English was so good that he was able to warn Fry: 'better not touch the hull, pal. It's still hot.' His purpose, he explained, was to persuade Fry to write a book warning earth men about prospects of a future nuclear war.

In *The Secret of the Flying Saucers* (1955) Orfeo Angelucci described making a flight to Neptune and discovering that he had been one of the space aliens in a previous existence. Howard Menger, in *From Outer Space to You* (1959) enlivens his account of aliens with descriptions of a number of

On the day after George Adamski died, April 24, 1965, a retired prison officer named E.A. Bryant had a curious encounter with a UFO. He was walking near Dartmoor about 5.30 pm when a flying saucer appeared out of thin air and swung back and forth like clock pendulum before coming to rest and hovering above the ground. An opening appeared in the side and three figures dressed in diving-suits came out. One beckoned to Bryant and as he approached, they removed their head gear. Two had fair hair and blue eyes, and foreheads that seemed too high to be merely human. The third was dark and had an ordinary human face.

The dark one talked to Bryant in foreign accented English, and apparently said that his name was 'Yamski', and that he wished someone called 'Des' or 'Les' was there to see him because he would understand everything. He explained that he and the others were from the planet Venus. After the UFO took off, some metallic fragments were found on the ground near the place where it had been.

The report of the experience led UFO-enthusiasts to speculate that the dark-haired visitor had been George Adamski – or his ghost – and that the 'Des' or 'Les' he referred to was his collaborator Desmond Leslie.

beautiful blondes, one of whom was over five hundred years old. Another contactee, Marian Keech, also claimed to have met beings from the planet Clarion, and Jesus – who had changed his name to Sananda – explained that he had also moved there. The purpose of the visit was to warn the earth people that a great flood was about to wipe out Salt Lake City, and all who wished to escape it should take to the higher ground. This prophecy seemed to echo the end-of-the-world prophecies of the 19th century – and, like them, was discredited when the disaster failed to occur.

One contactee called George King, a London taxi driver, described how he was alone in his flat when he was told that he was going to become the voice of an Interplanetary Parliament. After several trips to Mars and Venus, and saving the earth from destruction by helping to intercept a meteor, he moved to California, where his Aetherius Society has become one of the most successful organisations of its kind.

Yet some alien contacts had what would later be recognised as the stamp of authenticity. On 22 March, 1953, two lesbians who preferred to call themselves Sarah Shaw and Jan Whitley saw a bright light sweeping back and forth across their house in Tujunga Canyon, California. As Sarah knelt on the bed to peer out of the window, she felt giddy and confused. When she looked at the clock again, she realised that more than two hours had gone past, and that it was now after four in the morning.

It was not until 1975 when Sarah agreed to hypnosis that she recalled that she and Jan had been taken from their cabin and floated up through the air on to a UFO. There they were undressed and examined by black clad aliens who told Sarah that vinegar was a cure for cancer. Sarah apparently enjoyed the attentions she received from the male aliens. They were then 'floated' back to their cabin, where they lost all memory of the encounter.

Although the 'psychic investigator' Scott Rogo was to conclude that the symbolic rape was due to Sarah's unconscious dissatisfaction with her lesbian relationship, the events followed the pattern that would be later described by a great many UFO 'abductees'. The Sarah and Jan case seems to be the first on record.

On 21 August, 1955, Billy Ray Taylor and his wife June were visiting their friend Elmer Sutton on his farm near Hopkinsville, Kentucky. At about seven o'clock in the evening, Billy went out into the yard to fetch a drink from the well and saw a strange craft, 'real bright, but with an exhaust all the colours of the rainbow' land in a gulch nearby. Oddly enough, the Sutton family failed to be excited by his report, and no-one bothered to go outside.

An hour later, they were all alerted by the barking of the dog to the presence of an intruder near the farm-house, and saw 'a small glowing man with extremely large eyes, his arms extended over his head.' The two Sutton men fired at him with a rifle and shotgun and there was a sound 'as if I'd shot into a bucket', and the spaceman turned and hurried off. When another visitor appeared at the window the rifle was again fired and they ran outside to see if the creature had been hit. As one of them stopped under a low portion of the roof, a claw-like hand reached down from it and touched his hair. More shots were fired at the creature on the roof, and although it was hit directly it floated to the ground and hurried away. For the next three hours the eleven occupants of the house remained behind bolted doors frequently seeing the 'spacemen' at the windows. Finally, they rushed out of the house, piled into two cars, and drove to the nearest police-station in Hopkinsville. The police who returned with them could find no sign of the spacemen, but as soon as they were gone the creatures re-appeared. The next day, a police artist got witnesses to describe what they had seen; the picture that emerged were of tiny creatures with egg-shaped heads, very large yellow eyes spaced wide apart, and huge elephant-like ears. Their long thin arms ended in claw-like hands. They had slim, straight silvery bodies that seemed to be lit from the inside. This inner light, the Suttons said, intensified whenever they were shot at or even shouted at.

In spite of the derision that their story aroused when reported in the press, the Suttons — and the Taylors — continued to insist on its truth, and serious investigators who questioned them had no doubt whatever that they were not inventing their story.

One of the most famous of all cases of UFO 'contacts' is the story of Barney and Betty Hill. On 19 September, 1961, the couple began their drive from the Canadian border down through New Hampshire, returning from a holiday. Theirs was a mixed marriage, Barney being black and Betty white; they had both been Civil Rights workers.

As they drove along, Betty noticed that a bright object near the moon, which she had assumed to be a star or planet, was getting bigger. When she pointed it out to Barney, he commented that it was probably an artificial satellite.

Now, as they drove south through deserted country, the object appeared to be keeping up with them, travelling to the right of their car. It was blinking with multi-coloured lights. Finally, it was so close that it seemed to be huge, and the blinking lights had changed to a white glow. Finally, Barney stopped the car, and gazed at it through the binoculars. The object was now enormous, and they could see that it had a double row of windows. Barney stopped the car in the middle of the road and got out. Standing at the side of the road, he could see through the windows of the craft, and observed at least half a dozen people who appeared to be staring down at him.

Then all but one of them left the windows. Suddenly Barney had a conviction that he was about to be captured, and turned and ran for the car. As they accelerated away down the road, they could see no sign of the UFO. Barney suspected this was because the craft was directly overhead.

At this point they began to hear an electronic beeping noise which made the car vibrate. Suddenly both began to feel a curious sense of drowsiness, followed by a kind of dull haze.

When they recovered from this drowsiness, they saw a signpost pointing to Concord, which was seventeen miles away. Neither of them registered the fact that Concord was thirty-five miles away from Indian Head, where they had seen the UFO.

When they arrived home in Portsmouth, the dawn was rising, and their watches had both stopped. But their kitchen clock showed that it was five o'clock. They ate a light breakfast and went straight to bed.

The next day, Barney was inclined to dismiss the whole thing, and became annoyed when Betty insisted on talking about it.

To check whether the car had picked up any kind of radiation, Betty approached it with a compass, and was surprised to find on the lid of the boot a dozen or more shiny circles. When the compass was brought close to them, its needle showed a strong reaction.

In spite of Barney's protests, she rang a local Air Force base, and told her story — Barney was reluctantly brought to the phone to tell his own version. The officer to whom they spoke was able to tell them that they had received a number of other reports of unidentified flying objects in the area.

Betty went to the local library and borrowed a book called *The Flying Saucer Conspiracy*, by Major Donald Keyhoe, which argued that the Air Force was actively trying to discredit all UFO sightings. Keyhoe had organised the National Investigations Committee on Aerial Phenomena in Washington, to correlate and analyse every available UFO sighting. Betty wrote Major Keyhoe a letter, describing their experience – and describing the craft they had seen: 'It appeared to be pancake in shape, ringed with windows in the front through which we could see bright blue-white lights. Suddenly, two red lights appeared on each side. By this time my husband was standing in the road, watching closely. He saw wings protrude on either side and the red lights were on the wings tips.'

As a consequence of her letter, the Hills were visited by Walter Webb, a lecturer on the staff of the Hayden Planetarium in Boston. Webb was thoroughly sceptical when he set out on the drive, but after interviewing the Hills for several hours, he was totally convinced that they were telling the truth. Webb subsequently reported to the National Investigations Committee (NICAP) that he was totally convinced that their experience was genuine.

It was when they were repeating their story to a team of three men from NICAP that Barney and Betty Hill became clearly aware that a large section of time seemed to be missing from their drive that night. It was the time between the first occasion when they heard the beeping noise (which induced sleepiness) to the time they again heard the same beeping noise, and noticed the signpost pointing to Concord. The NICAP investigators suggested that it might be worth while placing the Hills under hypnosis to see whether they could somehow remember this lost period of time.

During the next year, the Hills returned several times to Indian Head in an attempt to remember precisely what had happened. Always, they ran up against the same amnesia after hearing the first series of beeps. Betty began to suffer from appalling nightmares, while Barney began to show signs of increasing nervous strain. It was after relating their story to a church discussion group in September 1963 that the Hills finally decided to consult a well known Boston psychiatrist, Doctor Benjamin Simon.

On 4 January, 1964, Barney Hill was placed under hypnosis by Doctor Simon and taped. Now he was able to remember what had happened after the first series of beeps. Their car had been blocked by a group of humanoids with large eyes, no nose, and slitty lipless mouths. Barney said they reminded him of red-haired, round-faced Irishmen. They were both taken on board the spacecraft – apparently in a kind of trance – and made to lie down on operating tables. Betty had to remove her dress, and a large needle was inserted into her navel – one of the humanoids, speaking English, told her that he was testing her for pregnancy.

The humanoids seemed very curious about human beings – they wanted to know precisely what they ate and drank, and were intrigued by the fact that Barney's teeth came out whereas hers did not. Finally, they were taken back to their car, and the spacecraft took off. It glowed with an orange colour, then rolled 'like a ball' and vanished into the dark sky.

On the tape, the Hills are at first able to remember exactly what has happened, and Betty asks her husband 'well, now try to tell me you don't believe in flying saucers.' But north of Concord, their memory blurs and then vanishes.

Oddly enough, although the accounts by Barney and Betty Hill were basically identical, Doctor Simon concluded that their description of going on board the spacecraft was purely imaginary, induced by their alarm at seeing a UFO. (Pease Air Force Base reported that radar had shown a UFO in the air at about the time that the Hills had their encounter.)

Barney Hill died of a cerebral haemorrhage in 1969. Betty Hill continued to reject the notion that what had happened on board the spacecraft was pure imagination.

Perhaps the most bizarre of all contact incidents occurred four years before the experience of Betty and Barney Hill. It happened in Brazil on 15 October, 1957. A twenty-three year old farmer called Antonio Villas Boas was ploughing the fields after dark, using his tractor headlights, when he saw 'a large red star' swooping down out of the sky. It was egg-shaped, and its lights illuminated the whole field. The dome of the machine was spinning anti-clockwise, and its colours changed from red to green as it slowed down to land. As Antonio tried to drive away in his tractor, the engine stopped. He jumped out of the tractor and started to run, but after only a few steps was grabbed by the arm. He pushed this creature to the ground, but was immediately grabbed by three others. He was then carried to their machine, which was standing about two metres above the ground on three metal supports. The aliens had considerable difficulty in dragging their captive up a narrow metal ladder, and into the machine. There, Boas was undressed by five of the aliens, who conversed in a strange language he could not understand. He was then taken into a smaller room, and when the door closed behind him, it disappeared, leaving only a wall. A rubber tube with some kind of a nozzle at the end was applied to his chin, and he saw his blood running down into a cup. After this he was bled on the other side of his chin. (Both bleedings left scars.)

Later, 'a noise at the door made me jump up with a start. I turned in that direction and had a tremendous surprise. The door was open and a woman was entering, walking in my direction. She came slowly, unhurriedly, perhaps amused at the surprise that must have been written on my face. I was flabbergasted, and not without good reason. The woman was stark naked, as naked as I was, and barefoot too.

'Moreover she was beautiful, though of a different type from the women I had known. Her hair was fair, almost white (like hair bleached with peroxide) smooth, not very abundant, reaching to halfway down her neck and with the ends curling inwards; and parted at the centre. Her eyes were large and blue, more elongated than round, being slanted outwards (like the slit eyes of those girls who make themselves up fancifully to look like Arabian princesses; that is how they were with the difference that here the thing was natural, there was no make-up whatever) . . .

'Her body was much more beautiful than that of any woman I have ever known before. It was slim, with high well-separated breasts, thin waist and small stomach, wide hips and large thighs. Her feet were small, her hands long and narrow, and her fingers and nails were normal. She was quite a lot shorter than I, her head reaching up to my shoulder.

'This woman came towards me silently, looking at me with the expression of someone wanting something, and she embraced me suddenly and began to rub her head from side to side against my face. At the same time I felt her body all glued to mine and also making movements . . .

'The door was closed again, leaving me alone there with that woman embracing me and giving me clearly to understand what she wanted, and I began to get excited . . . This seems incredible in the situation in which I found myself. I think that the liquid that they had rubbed onto my skin was the cause of this. They must have done it purposely. All I know is that I became uncontrollably excited, sexually, a thing that had never happened to me before. I ended up by forgetting everything and I caught hold of the woman, responded to her caresses with other and greater caresses . . . It was a normal act and she behaved just as any other woman would, as she did yet again, after more caresses. Finally she was tired and breathing rapidly. I was still keen but she was now refusing, trying to escape to avoid me, to finish with it all. When I noticed this I cooled off too. That was what they wanted of me – a good stallion to improve their own stock. In the final count that is all it was. I was angry, but then I resolved to pay no importance to it . . .

'One thing that I noticed was that she never kissed me even once. At a certain moment I recall that she opened her mouth as though she was going to do so, but it ended up with a gentle bite on my chin, which shows that it was not a kiss.'

After this, he was taken on a guided tour of the spacecraft, and tried unsuccessfully to steal an instrument as a keepsake – it weighed two kilos. Then he was allowed to climb back down the ladder on to the ground. 'The lights of the metal spurs and of the head-lamps and of the revolving dish all became brighter, while the dish was spinning faster and faster. Slowly the craft began to rise vertically. At that moment, the three shafts of the tripod on which it had been standing rose towards the sides, the lower part of each leg (narrower, rounded, and ending in an enlarged foot) began to enter the upper part which was much thicker and square, and when that was finished the top parts began to enter the base of the machine. Finally there was no longer anything to be seen there; the base was smooth and polished as though that tripod had never existed. I did not manage to make out any marks indicating the places where the shafts had fitted in.'

After this the craft took off moving at a great speed, and abruptly changing direction at one point. Then it shot off like a bullet towards the south. Boas estimated that he had been inside the spacecraft for more than four hours.

Boas was subsequently examined by a doctor who said that he had been subjected to radiation. The 'scars' were still on his chin.

Twenty years later, Boas appeared on Brazillian television, now a lawyer – he had been taking university

Albert K. Bender, who founded the International Flying Saucer Bureau, and who disbanded it in 1953, claimed that he had done so after an interview with a 'spaceman' who warned him that he would be killed if he continued to delve into the mystery of flying saucers.

Seven years later, Bender finally told the story, and also said that he asked the space being – whom he called the 'Exalted One' – various questions. Asked if he believed in God, the Exalted One replied that 'they' had no need to believe in things as earth people did. Asked if there was life on Mars, he said that there had been, but it was destroyed by invaders. The Martians had built beautiful cities and developed vast canals, but had not been as technologically advanced at the time of their destruction as earth civilisation is now. According to the Exalted One, Venus was now developing life.

Asked by Bender if earth people would reach the moon, he was told 'yes'. Seven years later, the prophecy came true.

correspondence courses at the time of his 'abduction' – and happily married with four children.

Clearly, most of these incidents of 'close encounters of the third kind' (as UFO expert J. Allen Hynek labelled them) sound preposterous and unbelievable. According to Peter Brookesmith, George Adamski wrote the story of his encounter with the aliens as science fiction, and then when it was turned down, re-wrote it as a 'true story.' (Later, four of the witnesses withdrew their testimony.) In other cases, we are forced to dismiss a 'contact' incident on circumstantial grounds. Farmer Gary T. Wilcox, of New York State, described how the hooded inhabitants of a cigar-shaped craft landed in a field while he was ploughing and told him 'do not be alarmed. We are from what you people refer to as the planet Mars.' This was in April 1964, long before it was known that Mars was unable to support any kind of life.

On the other hand, many of the descriptions of 'close encounters' are so similar that they give rise to the suspicion that the 'contactees' have read accounts of previous encounters. Yet in some cases, this seems to be virtually impossible. On 24 April, 1964, Patrolman Lonie Zamora, of Socorro, New Mexico, saw a strange flame in the sky, and then saw a large shiny object in a gully near the road. It was shaped rather like an egg balancing on one of its ends, and seemed to be standing on metal legs. Two small beings – who might have been children – in white overalls were standing near it. By the time Zamora had radioed back to his sergeant in Socorro, the visitors seem to have become aware of his presence, and the object took off with a roar that increased in volume, and vanished at a great speed in a south westerly direction. The brush where it had landed was still burning an hour later when Zamora brought back two colleagues to examine the spot. There were also four V-shaped depressions between one and two inches deep on the ground, each one about eighteen inches long.

Just over a year later, on 1 July, 1965, a French farmer called Maurice Masse, who lived in the Provencal village of Valensole, heard a whistling noise in the sky, and saw a craft shaped like a rugby football, which was standing on six legs with a central pivot stuck into the ground underneath it. There were also, he says, two 'boys of about eight years of age' standing near it.

Lights flying in formation above an air station in Massachussets, 1952

Suspecting that these were vandals who had been pulling up his lavender, he sneaked up on them until he became aware that they were not boys, whereupon he walked towards them. One of the two creatures pointed a pencil-like instrument at him and M. Masse was stopped in his tracks, unable to move. He described the creatures as less than four feet tall, with pumpkin-like heads, high fleshy cheeks, large eyes which slanted away around the sides of the face, slit mouths or holes without muscular lips and very pointed chins. They were dressed in close fitting grey-green clothes without anything over their heads. The two visitors then returned to their machine which took off. When the investigator Aime Michel went to talk to M. Masse, he took with him a colour photograph of a model spacecraft which had been reconstructed from the description given by Lonie Zamora. At the end of M. Masse's description of his encounter, he showed him the photograph. 'The effect produced on him was fantastic. I had the impression that, on seeing the image, M. Masse was at his last gasp, as though he had just looked upon his own death. At first he thought somebody had photographed *his* machine. When he learned that this one had been seen in the United States by a policeman, he seemed relieved and said to me: "You see then that I wasn't dreaming, and that I am not mad."'

It is while describing this incident in his book *The Humanoids* that UFO expert Charles Bowen raises the speculation that some of these 'frightening, spooky creatures described by some witnesses could be some sort of *psychic projection.*' 'Is it possible that *something* from *somewhere* is coming here, and by means incomprehensible to us — although it could be by a form of radiation as in radar waves — is pumping stylised pictures into the minds of humans who inadvertently stumble upon solid enough objects surreptitiously going about their business?'

'The psychic' explanation would be raised by many later investigators. The theory seems to be supported by the fact that Gary T. Wilcox's 'men from Mars' predicted the death of two Soviet cosmonauts and of US astronauts John Glenn and Gus Grissom within the year. In fact, Gus Grissom *did* die in a space accident, but this was in January 1967, three years later. It has been noted many times by mediums who believe that they are in contact with the dead that 'spirits' are able to foretell the future, but have no sense of time, so that their forecasts often take place sooner or later than they predict.

It might also be observed that the craft seen by M. Masse left behind clear marks on the soil, where its 'feet' had been. M. Masse also noted that no lavender would grow on that spot afterwards.

Chapter Three

WHO ARE THEY?

In 1960, a book called *The Morning of the Magicians* (Le Matin des Magiciens) by Louis Pauwels and Jacques Bergier, became an unexpected best seller in France, and then all over the world. It was a strange and bewildering book, which discussed alchemy, astrology, the Great Pyramid, Atlantis, black magic, mediumship, telepathy, and the ideas of Charles Fort. The book has many inaccuracies, typical of which is the assertion that 'in the middle of the 19th century a Turkish naval officer, Piri Reis, presented the Library of Congress with a set of maps which he had discovered in the east . . .' In fact, Piri Re'is was a Turkish pirate (although Re'is means admiral), who had been beheaded in 1554, and who had made his *own* map of the Atlantic — showing the South Pole and the coast of South America — and who admitted that he had pasted his map on twenty old maps, some of them from the great library of Alexandria, destroyed by invading Arabs in AD 640.

Still, in spite of its faults, the sheer range of its conjecture is exciting. In discussing the famous lines drawn on the desert in Nazca, Peru, the authors suggest that the makers of the lines may have been guided by some sort of machine floating in the sky. They go on to 'a Professor Mason', who refers to "the pre-Inca mythology, according to which the stars are inhabited, and the Gods have come down from the constellation of the Pleiades." They go on to state that they do not reject the possibility of visits from the inhabitants of other worlds. And they conclude the discussion of the Piri Re'is map: "Were these copies of still earlier maps? Had they been traced from observations made on board a flying machine or space vessel of some kind? Notes taken by visitors from Beyond?"

Bergier and Pauwels did not pursue their theory — at least, not in this book. But they could not have imagined the tremendous influence of their casual observation about visitors from other worlds.

The hint was taken up by a French writer named Robert Charroux, who, in 1964, produced a book called *Legacy of the Gods*, in which he argues that the 'angels' of the bible were actually visitors from other worlds. It obviously owes a great deal to *The Morning of the Magicians*, and, like that book, is full of strange and remote pieces of learning. Unsurprisingly, it failed to make the same impact as *Morning of the Magicians*.

In England, a retired Cambridge don named Tom Lethbridge became intrigued with the problem of flying saucers, and to whether our planet might have been visited by aliens in the remote past. Lethbridge was a skilful dowser, who had noticed that there seems to be some powerful earth force in the area of great stone megaliths like Stonehenge. He was also intrigued by the statement in the Book of Genesis: 'There were giants in the earth in those days . . .' And the comment that when the sons of God 'came unto the daughters of men, and they bare children to them, the same became mighty men which were of old . . .' There was also the legend of the 'war in heaven' in which Michael and his angels fought against a dragon. As an archaeologist, Lethbridge had studied some of the great figures of giants and dragons carved in chalk on the landscape. Could these legends, he wondered, reflect events that had really taken place in the remote past?

Moreover, since many of the megaliths — like Stonehenge and the great stones of Carnac, in Brittany — are remote from the sea, where they might have served as landmarks for sailors, could they have been intended to be visible *from the air* — to serve as guides to some kind of aircraft. Aware that these great stones seem to be charged with some kind of earth force, Lethbridge speculated whether they might be beacons to enable visitors from space to home in on their settlements. He introduced these strange speculations into the last book to be completed before his death, *The Legend of the Sons of God*.

Lethbridge had just completed his book when a friend handed him a copy of *Chariots of the Gods?* by the Swiss writer Erich von Daniken, and he was shattered to realise that Daniken had already proposed some of these ideas. For a few days he was tempted to destroy his own book, then decided that there were so many points of difference that this would be a pity. He concluded that the coincidence was 'an interesting example of the often observed phenomenon of a particular idea occurring to people in different parts of the world at the same time, just as if it had been put into their heads from outside.'

In fact, Daniken's book — whose German title means *Memories of the Future* — had already become an international best seller. Daniken had recognised that the best way to present controversial ideas is to state them dogmatically in words of one syllable. His book begins: 'It took courage to write this book, and it will take courage to read it.' Neither statement is true, but it gives the reader a sense of instant involvement. Daniken quickly goes on to state his main thesis: 'Nevertheless, one thing is certain . . . the past teemed with unknown Gods who visited the primeval earth in manned spaceships. Incredible technical achievements existed in the past. There is a mass of know-how which we have only partially rediscovered today.'

Daniken weaves his theories out of the familiar materials: 'The Great Pyramid, the Nazca lines in Peru, the ancient legends of giants and gods, the Piri Reis map. An American professor, Charles Hapgood, had become so intrigued by the Piri Reis map, and other maps dating from the middle

The statues of Easter Island

ages, that he had given them to his students as a study project. They had reached some remarkable conclusions – for example, that the South Pole, as shown in the Piri Reis map, had been drawn *before the Pole was covered with ice*, which must have been at least 6,000 years ago, and possibly as many as 9,000. Daniken makes full use of such strange anomalies. But he also adds a great deal of speculation, a mass of unassimilated facts, and some downright inventions. He takes from George Hunt Williamson the idea that the pyramids were built by spacemen – on the grounds that they are too massive to have been built by human beings; but he somehow manages to multiply their weight by five. He explains that the engineering problems would have been beyond men who knew nothing about the use of rope – although there are rope-making scenes on the walls of Egyptian tombs dating long before the building of the Great Pyramid. He suggests that the Nazca lines are giant runways, without pausing to reflect that even the most powerful modern aircraft does not need a runway several miles long. (In any case, the lines drawn on the desert are only scratched on its surface, and would quickly be blown in all directions if a plane attempted to land on them.)

At times, his information seems to be wilfully distorted. Chapter 5 of *Chariots of the Gods?* begins with an account of the Assyrian *Epic of Gilgamesh*, 'a sensational find that was made in the hill of Kuyundjik around the turn of the century.' (In fact, the *Epic* was discovered by Hormuzd Rassam, an assistant of the great archaeologist Layard, in 1853, and further missing portions were unearthed twenty years later). The aim of Daniken's re-telling is to demonstrate that the ancient races of Messopotania knew about space ships; so he describes how the sun god seized the hero Enkidu in his claws and bore him upward with such velocity that his body felt as heavy as lead – which, as Daniken rightly observes, seems to show an astonishing knowledge of the effect of acceleration. A visit to the tower of the goddess Ishtar (Innanis) is described, implying that it is a space vehicle, and then 'the first eye witness account of a spaceship' in which Enkidu flies for four hours in the brazen talons of an eagle and describes the earth as seen from the air.

Anyone who takes the trouble to check the Gilgamesh *Epic* will discover that all these episodes appear to have been imagined by Daniken: nothing remotely resembling them is to be found in it. The sun god (Shamash) does not seize Enkidu in his talons; there is no visit to the tower of the goddess Ishtar (she only makes one appearance in the *Epic* as the attempted seductress of Gilgamesh); there is no four hour space trip in the claws of an eagle.

Daniken also tells us that 'the door spoke like a living person', and that we can unhesitatingly identify this with a loud speaker; he goes on to say that Gilgamesh asks whether Enkidu has been smitten by the poisonous breath of a heavenly beast (i.e. has breathed in the fumes of a spaceship), and asks how Gilgamesh could possibly know that a 'heavenly beast' could cause fatal and incurable desease. The answer is that he couldn't, for he does not ask the question; neither does the loud speaker doorway make any kind of appearance in Gilgamesh.

Josef F. Blumrich, a Nasa space engineer who had spent most of his life designing and building aircraft and rockets – among them the giant Saturn V rocket – was irritated with Erich von Daniken's idea that what the prophet Ezekiel had seen was a UFO, and set out to refute him. Incredibly, he himself became a convert, and worked out a reconstruction of the spacecraft he thought Ezekiel had seen, including details of how it might have been operated.

Daniken's books provide, to put it kindly, plenty of examples of intellectual carelessness combined with wishful thinking and a casual attitude towards logic. In *Gold of the Gods*, he offers a photograph of a skeleton carved out of stone and wants to know: 'Were there anatomists who dissected bodies for the prehistoric sculptor? As we know, Wilhelm Conrad Rontgen did not discover the new kind of rays he called X-rays until 1895!' It never seems to have occurred to him that every graveyard must have been full of skeletons.

Perhaps the most obvious example of his carelessness was his treatment of Easter Island. Daniken alleged that the island's gigantic statues – some of them twenty feet high – could only have been carved and erected with the aid of sophisticated technology, which would have been far beyond the resources of primitive savages. In fact, the Norwegian explorer Thor Heyerdahl persuaded modern Easter Islanders to carve and erect statues with their own 'primitive technology'. Von Daniken had also pointed out that Easter Island has no wood for rollers – unaware that only a few centuries ago, the island was covered with woodland, and that the Easter Islanders have been responsible for the destruction of their own environment.

The von Daniken bubble finally burst in 1972, when, in *Gold of the Gods*, the author claimed to have visited a vast underground cave system in Ecuador, with elaboratly engineered walls, and examined an ancient library engraved on metal sheets. When his fellow explorer Juan Moricz, denied that von Daniken had ever entered the caves, von Daniken admitted that his account was fictional, but argued that his book was not intended to be a scientific treatise; since it was designed for popular consumption, he had allowed himself a certain degree of poetic license. Yet in a biography of Daniken, Peter Krassa ignores this admission, insisting that the case is still open and that Daniken may have been telling the truth after all.

In fact, a British expedition to the caves found them to be natural, with evidence of habitation by primitive man but with no signs of Daniken's ancient library or perfectly engineered walls. A two hour T.V. expose of von Daniken subsequently punctured every one of his major claims.

The Dogon

Yet in spite of Daniken's absurdities, it has to be admitted that there *is* a certain amount of evidence for the 'ancient astronaut' theory. Members of an African tribe called the Dogon, who live in the Republic of Mali, some 300 miles south of Timbuktu, insist that they possess knowledge that was transmitted to them by 'spacemen' from the star Sirius, which is 8.7 light-years away. Dogon mythology insists that the 'Dog Star' Sirius (so-called because it is in the constellation Canis) has a dark companion that is invisible to the naked eye, and that is dense and very heavy. This is correct; Sirius does indeed have a dark companion known as Sirius B.

The existence of Sirius B. had been suspected by astronomers since the mid-nineteenth century, and it was first observed in 1862 – although it was not described in detail until the 1920s. Is it possible that some white traveller took the knowledge of Sirius B. to Africa sometime since the 1850s? It is possible but unlikely. Two French anthropologists, Marcelle Griaule and Germaine Dieterlen, first revealed the 'secret of the Dogon' in an obscure paper in 1950; it was entitled 'a Sudanese Sirius System' and was published in the *Journal de la Sociate des Africainistes*.

The two anthropologists had lived among the Dogon since 1931, and in 1946 Griaule was initiated into the religious secrets of the tribe. He was told that fish-like creatures called the Nommo had come to earth from Sirius to civilise its people. Sirius B., which the Dogon call *Po Tolo* (naming it after the seed that forms the staple part of their diet, and whose botanical name is *Digitaria*), is made of matter heavier than any on earth and moves in an eliptical orbit, taking fifty years to do so. It was not until 1928 that Sir Arthur Eddington postulated the theory of 'white dwarfs' – stars whose atoms have collapsed inward, so that a piece the size of a pea could weigh half a ton. (Sirius B. is the size of the earth yet weighs as much as the sun.) Griaule and Dieterlen went to live among the Dogon three years later. Is it likely that some traveller carried a new and complex scientific theory to a remote African tribe in the three years between 1928 and 1931?

An oriental scholar named Robert Temple went to Paris to study the Dogon with Germaine Dieterlen. He soon concluded that the knowledge shown by the Dogon could not be explained away as coincidence or 'defusion' (knowledge passed on through contact with other peoples). The Dogon appeared to have an extraordinarily detailed knowledge of our solar system. They said that the moon was 'dry and dead', and they drew Saturn with a ring around it (which, of course, is only visible through a telescope). They knew that the planets revolved around the sun. They knew about the moons of Jupiter (first seen through a telescope by Galileo). They had recorded the movements of Venus in their temples. They knew that the earth rotates and that the number of stars is infinite. And when they drew the eliptical orbit of Sirius, they showed the star off-centre, not in the middle of the orbit – as someone without knowledge of astronomy would naturally conclude.

The Dogon insist that their knowledge was brought to them by the amphibious Nomo from a 'star' (presumably they meant a planet) which, like Sirius B., rotates around Sirius and whose weight is only a quarter of Sirius B's. They worshipped the Nomo as gods. They drew diagrams to portray the spinning of the craft in which these creatures landed and were precise about the landing location as the place to the north-west of present Dogon country, where the Dogon originated. They mentioned that the 'ark' in which the Nomo arrived caused a whirling dust storm and that it 'skidded'. They speak of 'a flame that went out as they touched the earth', which implies that they landed in a small space capsule. Dogon mythology also mentions a glowing object in the sky like a star, presumably the mother ship. Our telescopes have not yet revealed the 'planet' of the Nomo, but that is hardly surprising. Sirius B. was only discovered because its weight caused perturbations in the orbit of Sirius. The Dog Star is 35.5 times as bright (and hot) as our sun, so any planet capable of supporting life would have to be in the far reaches of its solar system and would almost certainly be invisible to telescopes. Temple surmises that the planet of the Nomo would be hot and steamy and that this probably explains why intelligent life evolved in its seas, which would be cooler. These fish-people would spend much of their time on land but close to the water; they would need a layer of water on their skins to be comfortable, and if their skins dried, it would be as agonising as severe sunburn. Temple sees them as a kind of dolphin.

But what were such creatures doing in the middle of the desert near Timbuktu? In fact, the idea is obviously absurd. Temple points out that to the northwest of Mali lies Egypt, and for many reasons, he is inclined to believe that the landing of the Nomo took place there. Temple also points out that a Babylonian historian named Berossus – a contemporary and apparently an aquaintance of Aristotle (4th century BC) – claims in his history, of which only fragments survive, that Babylonian civilisation was founded by alien amphibians, the chief of whom is Oannes – the Philistines knew him as Dagon (and the science fiction writer H.P. Lovecraft borrowed him for his own mythology). The Greek Gramarian Apollodorus (about 140 BC) had apparently read more of Berossu, for he criticises another Greek writer, Abydenus, for failing to mention that Oannes was only one of the 'fish-people'; he calls these aliens 'annedoti' ('repulsive ones') and says they are 'semi-demons' from the sea.

Why should the Dogon pay any particular attention to Sirius, even though it was one of the brightest stars in the sky? After all, it was merely one of thousands of stars. There, at least, the sceptics can produce a convincing answer. Presumably, the Dogon learned from the Egyptians, and for the ancient Egyptians, Sothis (as they called Sirius) was the most important star in the heavens – at least after 3200 BC, when it began to rise just before the dawn, at the beginning of the Egyptian new year, and signalled that the Nile was about to rise.

So the Dog Star became the god of the rising waters. The goddess Sothis was identified with Isis; and Temple points out that in Egyptian tomb paintings, Isis is usually to be found in a boat with two fellow goddesses, Anukis and Satis. Temple argues convincingly that this indicates that the Egyptians knew Sirius to be a three-star system – the unknown 'Sirius sea' being the home of the Nomo. An ancient Arabic name for one of the stars in the Sirian constellation (not Sirius itself) is Al Wazn, meaning 'wait', and one text said that it is almost too heavy to rise above the horizon.

Temple suggests that the ancients may have looked towards the Canis constellation for Sirius B. and mistaken it for Al Wazn. He also suggests that Homer's Sirens – mermaidlike creatures who are all-knowing and who try to lure men away from their everyday responsibilities – are actually 'Sirians', amphibious goddesses. He also points out that Jason's boat, the Argo, is associated with the goddess Isis and that it has fifty rowers – fifty being the number of years it takes Sirius B. to circle Sirius A. There are many other fish-bodied aliens in Greek mythology, including the Telchines of Rhodes, who were supposed to have come from the sea and to have introduced men to various arts, including metalwork. Significantly, they had dogs' heads.

But if the Egyptians knew about Sirius B. and the Nommo, then why do we not have Egyptian texts that tell us about aliens from the Dog Star system? Here the answer is obvious. Marcelle Grialle had to be 'initiated' by Dogon priests before he was permitted to learn about the visitors from Sirius. If the Egyptians knew about Sirius B., the knowledge was revealed only to initiates. But it would have left its mark in Egyptian mythology – for example, in the boat of Isis.

Temple's book *The Sirius Mystery* (1976) is full of such 'mythological evidence', and much of it has been attacked for stretching interpretation too far. Yet what remains when all the arguments have been considered is the curious fact that a remote African tribe has some precise knowledge of an entire star system not visible to the human eye alone and that they attribute this knowledge to aliens from that star system. That single fact suggests that in spite of Daniken's absurdities, we should remain open minded about the possibility of alien visitors who once landed on our planet.

Jung on Flying Saucers

In 1958, the psychologist Carl Jung entered the controversy with a book called *Flying Saucers: a Modern Myth of Things Seen in the Skies*. Jung's theory is that flying saucers are what he calls 'projections' – which is another name for illusions or hallucinations. He believes that these 'projections' originate in what he calls the 'collective unconscious' – that is, a deep stratum of the unconscious mind that is full of the basic myths and symbols of the human race. Jung sees great significance in the fact that flying saucers are circular – like mandalas – the Tibetan religious symbol of a 'mystic circle', which is also found in most religions of the world.

Dr. Carl Jung, Swiss Physician and Psychiatrist

UFOs

According to Jung, man has a religious craving – what he calls 'the religious function' – which is as deep as the sexual needs emphasised by Freud. This craving is basically a need for personal evolution, or what Jung calls 'individuation'. So, according to Jung, the flying saucer is basically a projection of modern man's craving for a saviour – for some kind of religious evolution.

But there is a complication; Jung admits that UFOs can be photographed and cause images on radar screens. Then how *can* they be 'projections' – if a projection is basically an illusion? Jung leaves that question unanswered; but he implies that under certain conditions, a 'projection' *can* cause physical effects. In other words, the mind can affect physical reality. But Jung is careful not to underline this aspect, and few of the comentaries on his book even mention it.

But one further complication is provided by an interview between Jung and the aviator Charles Lindbergh in the summer of 1959. 'To my astonishment', said Lindbergh (in a letter to his publisher's wife), 'I found that Jung accepted flying saucers as factual. On the one hand, he didn't seem in the least interested in psychological aspects. On the other, he didn't seem at all interested in factual information relating to the investigation of flying saucers reports.' When Lindbergh told Jung that the US Air Force had found no evidence whatever for flying saucers, 'it was obvious that he did not wish to pursue the subject further.' Lindbergh persisted, pouring cold water on the sightings, and quoting his friend General Spaatz (of the Us Air Force) as saying: 'Don't you suppose that if there was anything true about this flying saucer business, you and I would have heard about it by this time?' Jung's reply was: 'There are a great many things going on around this earth that you and General Spaatz don't know about.' It seems clear, then, that, as in so many other cases, Jung was telling slightly less than he knew when presenting his views to the public. Significantly, Lindbergh commented: 'One intuitively feels the elements of mysticism and greatness about him — even though they may have been mixed at times, with elements of charlatism.'

In June 1954, the Stratoliner of the British Overseas Airways Corporation was three miles out of New York, on its way to London, when Captain James H. Howard noticed a large elongated object and six smaller objects about three miles off on their left side.

As the plane approached Goose Bay, Canada, for re-fuelling, the large UFO seemed to change shape and the smaller ones converged on it. Then they seemed to disappear inside it, and the big one shrank.

Howard contacted the Ground Control and the US Airforce sent a Saber Fighter to the scene. Captain Howard did not see what happened, because he had to leave Goose Bay for London.

Howard, his co-pilot, and several passengers all confirmed the sighting of the UFO. But in 1968, the United States Airforce dismissed the sighting as 'an optical mirage phenomenon'.

Are They Fairies?

In 1970, a scientist named Jacques Vallee produced one of the most startling theories about UFOs so far. In a book called *Passport to Magonia*, Vallee pointed out the many similarities between 'close encounters' with flying saucers and those with fairies.

Before we go any further, it is important to recognise that the evidence for fairies – or 'the little people' – is in many ways as convincing as the evidence for flying saucers. The poet W.B. Yeats, born in Ireland, spent a great deal of time in the west of Ireland investigating stories about fairies, and soon recognised that the majority of Irish country folk accepted their existence as a concrete fact of life. Yeats himself ultimately came to believe in the real existence of the 'little folk'. He encouraged the orientalist W.Y. Evans Wentz – best known for his translation of *The Tibetan Book of the Dead* – to study the folklore of the fairies; the result was Wentz's first book, *The Fairy Faith in Celtic Countries* (1911), one of the best books on the subject. Yeat's friend, the poet AE (George Russell) contributed an anonymous piece to the book (under the title 'An Irish Mystic's Testimony') in which he described his own fairy sightings with a factual accuracy and precision of an anthropologist describing primitive tribes: shining beings, opalescent beings, water beings, wood beings, lower elementals:

'The first of (the fairies) I saw I remember very clearly . . . There was first a dazzle of light, and then I saw that this came from the heart of a tall figure with a body apparently shaped out of half-transparent or opalescent air, and throughout the body ran a radiant electrical fire, to which the heart seemed the centre. Around the head of this being and through its waving luminous hair, which was blown all about the body like living strands of gold, there appeared flaming wing-like auras. From the being itself light seemed to stream outwards in every direction; and the effect left on me after the vision was one of extraordinary lightness, joyousness or ecstasy.'

At the end of his book, Wentz concludes that the factual and scientific evidence for the real existence of fairies is overwhelming, that in fact 'there are hundreds of proven cases of phenomena'.

Many of the cases quoted by Wentz sound like cases of 'second sight', the ability to see 'spirits'. But there have been many fairy sightings that make them seem much more down to earth. A psychic called Lois Bourne, in her book *Witch Among Us* describes her own sighting of one of the 'little people' in Cornwall. During an evening with a member of a 'wicca' coven, she and her husband Wilfred were asked if she would like to see a goblin. The host explained that one appeared among the rushes of the mill stream at Treago Mill, Cuberts Heath, every morning at sunrise. If they wanted to see him, they would have to be up early. The next morning Lois and her husband joined their host at the mill gate and crept up the stream. She writes: 'I have never been able to decide, and still cannot decide, whether I really saw that goblin, or if Rob made me see it . . . Whatever it was there, sitting on a stone calmly washing his socks, was an elfin creature with a red hat, green coat and trews, one yellow sock on and the other one in his tiny hands, in the process of being washed. I remember thinking at the time, in my sleepy, befuddled, but practical way, "what an atrocious colour combination." Suddenly he saw us and he disappeared . . . "Now do you believe me?" asked Rob.'

Vallee tells how, at eleven o'clock on the morning of 18 April 1961, a sixty year old chicken farmer named Joe Simonton, who lived near Eagle River, Wisconsin, was attracted out of his house by a peculiar noise similar to 'nobby tyres on a wet pavement'. In his yard there was a silvery saucer-shaped object, brighter than chrome', which appeared to be hovering close to the ground without touching it. It was about twelve feet high and thirty feet in diameter. A hatch opened about five feet from the ground, and Simonton saw three men inside the machine.

UFOs

They were about five feet tall, and dressed in black. Simonton said they appeared to look like Italians.

One of them held up a jug made of chrome, and signalled to Joe Simonton that he needed water. Simonton filled it inside the house and when he returned, saw that one of the men inside the saucer was 'frying food on a flameless grill of some sort'. The interior of the ship was black. Simonton could see several instrument panels and heard a slow whining noise like the hum of a generator. When he made a motion indicating that he was interested in the food, one of the men who was also dressed in black handed him three cookies, about three inches in diameter and perforated with small holes. After a few minutes, the door closed in such a way that its outline was almost undetectable and the object arose twenty feet from the ground before taking off, causing a blast of air that bowed nearby trees.

Simonton went along to the offices of the Food and Drug Laboratory of the US Department of Health, Education and Welfare, and asked them to analyse one of the cookies. The laboratory concluded that the material was an ordinary pancake of terrestrial origin.

Two deputies sent by the sheriff, who had known Simonton for fourteen years, arrived at the scene but could not find any evidence of the saucer. But the sheriff commented that it was obvious that Simonton believed in the truth of what he was saying and talked very sensibly.

Vallee then goes on to talk about Wentz's book on the fairy faith, and quotes the story of Pat Feeney, who described how one day, a little woman came to his house and asked for oatmeal: 'Paddy had so little that he was ashamed to offer it, so he offered her some potatoes instead, but she wanted oatmeal, and then he gave her all that he had. She told him to place it back in the bin till she should return for it. This he did and the next morning the bin was overflowing with oatmeal. The woman was one of the Gentry.'

Like Yeats, Wentz was able to pick up dozens of factual accounts of the Gentry: 'When I was a young man I often used to go out in the mountains over there to fish for trout or hunt. And it was in January on a cold, dry day while carrying my gun that I and a friend with me as we were walking around Ben Bulben saw one of the Gentry for the first time . . . This one was dressed in blue with a head-dress adorned with what seemed to be frills. When he came upon us, he said to me in a sweet and silvery voice,

'The seldom you come to this mountain the better, Mister, a young lady here wants to take you away.'

Then he told us not to fire our guns, because the Gentry disliked being disturbed by the noise. And he seemed to be like a soldier of the Gentry on guard. As we were leaving the mountain, he told us not to look back and we didn't.'

Vallee also tells the strange story of the Madonna of Guadalupe. In 1531, a fifty-seven year old Aztec Indian called Singing Eagle, and whose Spanish name was Juan Diego, was going to church in Tlaltelolco, near Mexico City. Suddenly the air was full of sweet bird song, and since it was a freezing December morning, he was puzzled. Then someone with a harmonious voice called his name from the top of a hill. When he climbed the hill, he saw 'a young Mexican girl about fourteen years old and wonderfully beautiful.' There were golden beams around her, although the sun was still below the horizon. She told Juan Diego that her name was Mary, and she wanted a temple at that particular place: 'so run now to Tenochtitlan (later Mexico City) and tell the Lord Bishop all that you have seen and heard.'

In great embarrassment the poor Indian went to the Bishop's palace. He succeeded in gaining an audience with the Bishop, but, just as he expected, the Bishop obviously thought he was mad. On his way home he once again met the lady, and told her that he should send a more suitable messenger. She replied that she had chosen him, and that he had to go back to the Bishop again the next day. 'Tell him it is the Virgin Mary who sends you.'

Juan Diego went back to the Bishop's Palace the next day, and the Bishop, whose name was Fray Juan de Zumarraga was impressed by his air of honesty. He told Juan to ask the apparition for some sign, and then told two servants to follow him secretly. They followed him up the hill, at which point he vanished. (Vallee points out that this sounds exactly like a traditional fairy tale, with a human being vanishing into a fairy hill.)

In fact, Juan saw the lady again, and told him to come back the following day at day-break, when he would be given a sign for the Bishop. However, the next morning, Juan's uncle – his only relative – was seriously ill, and Juan spent the day trying to relieve his sufferings. As he set out to find a priest the following morning, he met the lady again, and when he explained why he had failed to keep the appointment, was relieved when she said: 'Are you not under my shadow and protection? Your uncle will not die this time. At this very moment his health is restored. There is now no reason for your journey and you can peacefully attend to mine. Go to the top of the hill, cut the flowers you will find there, and bring them to me.' And at the top of the hill, on a mid-winter day, Juan found Castilian roses, 'their petals wet with dew'. He placed these in his Indian cape (*tilma*). The lady arranged the flowers in his cape, then tied it behind his neck so the roses would not fall out.

At the Bishop's palace, the servants made fun of Juan, but when they tried to grab some of the roses, they were baffled as the flowers seemed to dissolve in their fingers. Eventually, Juan was allowed to see the Bishop. As he untied his tilma, the flowers fell in an untidy heap on the floor, but this was evidently not the sign that the lady had intended. The tilma now had a beautiful picture of the Virgin embroidered on it in bright colours. The bishop fell on his knees before it, and then followed Juan Diego to the hill where he had seen the Virgin. The church was accordingly built there – the hill is called Tepeyac – in her name, and above the altar, Juan Diego's tilma is still, after more than four centuries, as bright and unfaded as ever.

The natural tendency of the sceptic is to dismiss this as a story invented to explain a particularly beautiful piece of woven cloth. But Vallee is more concerned in pointing out the similarity of this 'myth' and so many sightings of 'little people' and UFOs. He also points that many other religious 'apparitions' bear a strong resemblance to UFOs hovering in the sky.

Vallee adds another interesting speculation to his story of Guadalupe Madonna. Why Guadalupe, which is a small town in a mountain range in Spain? Vallee suggests that the Indian word used by the apparition was *tetlcoatlaxopeuh*, which would be transcribed phonetically *deguatlashhupee*, which to a Spaniard would sound like 'de Guadalupe'. But the original word tetlcoatlaxopeuh means 'stone serpent trodden on'. The stone serpent – quetzalcoatl – is the image of the ancient Mayan god, so 'stone serpent trodden on' may mean that quetzalcoatl has been surplanted by the Christian religious symbol. The story unites the religion of ancient Mexico with modern Christianity. Vallee also points out that the sweet sound of birds heard by Juan Diego is like the 'sweet music' described so often in accounts of those who claim to have encountered the faery.

In a later book, *The Invisible College* (1975) later re-issued under the title of *UFOs: The Psychic Solution* (1977), Vallee expands his thesis about religious 'apparitions' to include those of Lourdes, Fatima and Knock. What Vallee appears to be saying is that UFO acitivity should not be taken as a simple material phenomenan, like meteorites. Like Jung, he feels that it is closely connected with the mentality of those who observe it. And just as a religious apparition can be interpreted into ways, (1) wishful thinking by religiously-inclined people and (2) a genuine intervention from the 'world of the spirit', so he feels that UFOs can be regarded as delusions or as some kind of 'intervention' whose purpose is connected with causing a change in human consciousness. He calls the last chapter of his book 'The Control System', and compares UFO sightings to the thermostats that regulate the temperature in our houses. 'I propose the hypothosis that there is a control system for human consciousness. I have not determined whether it is natural or spontaneous; whether it is explainable in terms of genetics, of social psychology, or of ordinary phenomena – or if it is artificial in nature, and under the power of some superhuman will. It may be entirely determined by laws that we have not yet discovered.'

Here, then, we have moved a long way from the simplistic view that UFOs are either manifestation of dangerous aliens who wish to colonise our earth, or that they are benevolent aliens who wish to educate the human race. Like Jung, Vallee appears to be suggesting that there is some form of 'other reality' – and that their purpose is to make human beings aware of some other level of reality.

John Keel on UFOs

John Keel is a New York journalist whose original attitude towards flying saucers was sceptical. But in 1953, in Egypt, he saw his first UFO, a metallic disc with a revolving rim hovering over the Aswan dam in daylight. Yet even so, it was not until 1966 that he decided to undertake a careful study of the subject, and subscribed to a press-cutting . . . (word missed). What then staggered him was the sheer number of the sightings – he often received a hundred and fifty clippings in a day. Moreover, it soon became clear that even these were only a small percentage of the total, and that thousands of sightings were going unrecorded. What also fascinated Keel was that so many witnesses who had

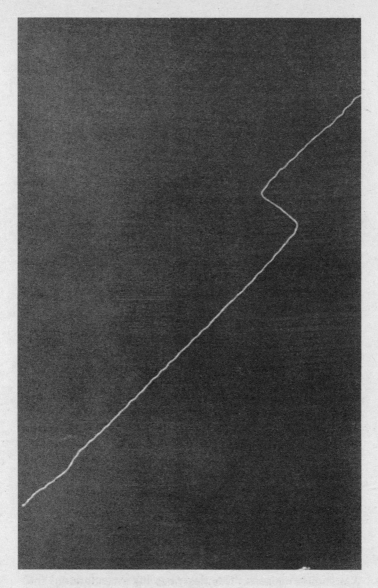

Trail left by a UFO in Texas, 1974

seen UFOs from their cars had later seen them over their homes; this suggested that the 'spacemen' were not merely alien scientists or explorers, engaged in routine surveying work, but that they took an active interest in the people with whom they made 'contact'. (A later student of UFOs, Bud Hopkins — whom we shall meet later — believes that the 'aliens' may maintain a relationship with generation after generation of 'contactees'.)

In 1967, Keel was driving along the Long Island expressway when he saw a sphere of light in the sky, presumably of course parallel to his own. When he reached Huntington, he found that cars were parked along the roads, and dozens of people were staring at four lights that were bobbing and weaving in the sky; the light that had followed Keel joined the other four. Keel was in fact on his way to interview a scientist, Phillip Burchhardt, who had seen a UFO hovering above some trees close to his home on the previous evening, and had examined it through binoculars; he had seen that it was a silvery disc illuminated by rectangular lights that blinked on and off.

Keel was impressed by the witnesses he interviewed; most were ordinary people who had no obvious reason for inventing a story about UFOs. His study of the actual literature convinced him that it was ninety-eight percent nonsense; but most individual witnesses were obviously telling the truth. Keel had soon accumulated enough cases to fill a two-thousand page typescript; this had to be severely truncated before it was published under the title *UFOs: Operation Trojan Horse*. As the title suggests, Keel was inclined to see the phenomenon as the beginning of some alien invasion. He concludes in a later book that 'our little planet seems to be experiencing the interpenetration of forces or entities from some other space-time continuum.'

The essence of Keel's views can be found in his book *The Mothman Prophesies*. This describes his investigations into various UFO sightings in West Virginia in 1966–67. He reports numerous sightings of a huge figure – about seven feet tall – with red eyes and gigantic wings folded on its back. It was able to keep up with fast cars without even flapping its wings. It was seen by two young couples near an old ammunition dump on 15 November, 1966, and again by a girl called Connie Carpenter twelve days later. Connie Carpenter's eyes became red and swollen, as if from some kind of radiation, after she had seen the creature's red eyes at close quarters. In the spring of the following year, a young couple making love naked in the back of a car, saw a large ball of bluish fire hovering near the car; the next morning, both were heavily 'sunburned' and had red swollen eyes. Keel's book is full of similar electronic oddities. Calls come through on disconnected telephones; police messages are picked up on switched-off radios; films and tape recordings turn out to be blank; cameras refuse to work when pointed at UFOs. Cows and sheep are found with their throats neatly slit and their bodies drained of blood. Pet dogs and cats disappear in large numbers. Keel found that his movements were actually anticipated by the opposition – for example, when he casually chose a motel to stay at, he found a sheaf of incomprehensible messages waiting for him at the desk.

According to himself, Keel was finally subjected to a kind of non-stop persecution by the 'spacemen', with mysterious phonecalls, people impersonating him or claiming to be his secretary, and strange warning messages. He was convinced that the spacemen were genuine because they were able to make accurate predictions of the future. When he hypnotised a contactee in 1967, a spaceman named 'Apol' began to speak through her, and made exact predictions about a number of plane crashes. Apol also predicted that the Pope would be knifed to death in the Middle East, and that this would be preceded by a great earthquake. He mentioned that Robert Kennedy was in great danger – Kennedy was of course assassinated in the following year.

The plane crashes, says Keel, occurred exactly as predicted. In July 1967, the Vatican announced that the Pope would be visiting Turkey, and an earthquake killed a thousand people there. But the Pope was not knifed to death at Istanbul Airport. It was three years later, when he landed at Manilla Airport that a madman tried to kill him with a long knife; fortunately the man was overpowered by guards. Keel believes that the entity simply mis-read the future or got the date wrong. Similarly, he was told that Martin Luther King would be shot in the throat while standing on his balcony in Memphis; the date given was 4 February, 1968. That day passed without incident; the assassination took place, exactly as described, two months later.

In long telephone conversations with Keel, 'Apol' made another prophesy; there would be a massive power failure that would affect a large part of the United States on December 15. It would happen when President Johnson turned on the lights of the Christmas tree on the White House lawn. Keel watched the event on television; there was no power faillure. But immediately after the President had thrown the switch, the programme was interrupted for an announcement − a bridge on the Ohio river had collapsed, with great loss of life. Keel knew that the only bridge along the stretch mentioned was the Silver Bridge at Point Pleasant, the town near which all the strange occurrences had been taking place. The spaceman had even warned him that a major disaster would strike along the Ohio river, but implied that it would be a factory that would blow up. Keel believes that they told him the blackout story, rather than the truth, so he would have no opportunity to warn people.

Keel continues to believe that the phenomena he has observed can be violent and extremely dangerous. In this he is echoed by the British expert on UFOs, Brinsley Le Poer Trench (the Earl of Clancarty), who reached a similar conclusion in his book *Operation Earth*:

Who Are They?

'. . . there exist at least two diametrically opposed forces of entities interested in us. Firstly, those that are the real Sky People who have been around since time immemorial. Secondly, those that live in an area indigenous to this planet, though some of us believe they also live in the interior of the earth. There is obviously a "War in the Heavens" between these two factions. However it is not considered that battles are going on in the sense that humans usually envisage them. It is more of a mental affray for the domination of the minds of mankind.'

Chapter Four

COVER-UP?

Project Blue Book

I n September 1947, the US Air Force launched an investigation of UFOs, which was at that time code named 'Project Sign'. In 1951, this became 'Project Blue Book'. It was located at the Right-Patterson Air Force Base in Dayton, Ohio, as part of the Air Technical Intelligence Centre (ATIC) and later the Foreign Technology Division (FTD). For much of this time, project Blue Book was under the direction of Doctor Edward Condon, of the University of Colorado. Project Blue Book was finally dropped by the Air Force in 1969, on Condon's recommendation – and after the publication of his Report.

In the late 1940s, the astronomer J. Allen Hynek was appointed as astronomical consultant to the US Air Force, and quickly became convinced that, whatever lay behind the UFO reports, they were undoubtedly not a hoax or a delusion. It was Hynek who classified UFO reports into four types: Close Encounters of the First Kind and of the Second and the Third Kind. Close Encounters of the First Kind are of the type in which the UFO is simply seen at close range. In the Second Kind, there is some physical effect left behind by the UFO – such as burnt grass. Close Encounters of the Third Kind, used as the title of the Steven Spielberg film, are cases in which the 'occupants' of the UFO are seen.

UFOs

Although a scientist himself, Hynek ended by being thoroughly critical of the attitude of scientists. He reports how, during an evening reception of several hundred astronomers in Victoria, British Columbia, in the summer of 1968, word spread through the hall that someone had seen manoeuvering lights outside. 'The news was met by casual banter and the giggling sound that often accompanies an embarrassing situation. *Not one astronomer ventured outside in the summer night to see for himself.* (My italics).

The main value of Hynek's book *The UFO Experience: A Scientific Enquiry* (1972) is that it is so highly critical of the Air Force investigation and the Condon Report, which, as he says, gave the 'kiss of death' to official UFO investigation. Condon had written: 'while we do not think at present that anything at present is likely to come out of such research, each individual case ought to be carefully considered on its own merits' — which Hynek describes as 'truly a masterpiece of throwing a scrap of political meat to the critic dogs.'

In fact, two members of Condon's team, David Saunders and Norman Levina embarrassed Condon by publishing a memorandum written by the project coordinator, Robert Low soon after it was initiated. This admitted: 'our study would be conducted almost exclusively by nonbelievers who, although they couldn't possibly *prove* a negative result, could and probably would add an impressive body of evidence *that there is no reality to the observations.* (My italics). The trick would be, I think, to describe the project so that to the public, it would appear a totally objective study, but to the scientific community, would present the image of a group of nonbelievers trying their best to be objective, but having an almost zero expectation of finding a saucer.' It goes on to recommend that the emphasis should be put on the psychology of the kind of people who report UFOs – in other words, suggests that these are nuts and cranks.

When this was published, Condon was furious and dismissed Saunders and Levina for insubordination.

The result, of course, is that most serious students of the UFO phenomenon take a sceptical and negative view of officialdom and its opinions.

This kind of scepticism seems to have been justified by the reaction to a flurry of UFO sightings in and around Exeter, New Hampshire, in the autumn of 1965. A Mrs Jalbert, with her four sons, saw a silvery object with bright flashing lights hovering near power lines near their home – occasionally an aircraft would pursue it. Two young people saw a UFO emerge from the sea at Hampton Beach which then pursued their car. A Mrs Bloggett saw a blinding ball of light rotating at high speed over the treetops. And at around 1.30 a.m. on 3 September 1965, a patrolman named Bertrand checked a parked car and was told by the distraught woman inside it that she had been followed for twelve miles by a huge, silent UFO, which had flown off at great speed. When he got back to the Police Station, the patrolman found an eighteen-year-old boy called Norman Muscarello, who declared that he had also seen a giant, silent UFO when he was hitch-hiking to his home in Exeter. He said that it was bigger than a house and appeared to be eighty or ninety feet in diameter, with brilliant, pulsating red lights around an apparent rim. He dived into a ditch, and the object moved away – after which he quickly hitched a lift into Exeter.

Muscarello and Patrolman Bertrand hurried back to the spot, where they found 'a group of five red lights . . . extremely bright (which) flashed on one at a time. The lights started to move around over the field. At one time, they came so close I fell to the ground and started to draw my gun . . . there was no sound or vibration but the farm

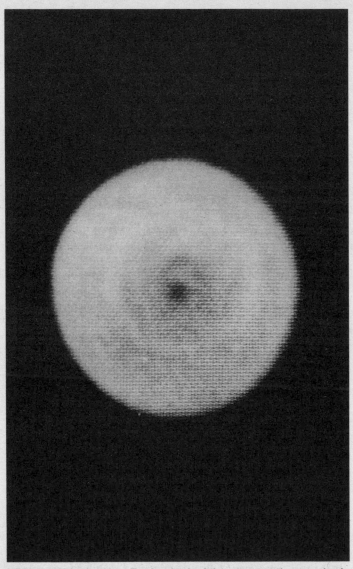

UFO spotted by a New Zealand television crew at the mouth of the Clarence River, 1979

animals were upset and making a lot of noise . . . I radioed
Patrolman David Hunt, who arrived in a few minutes. He
also observed the lights . . .'

But when all this was reported, investigators from Pease
Air Force Base pointed out that five B-47 Bombers were
airborne at the time of the sightings. Then, on 27 October,
the Pentagon issued a statement saying that the sightings
were due to aircraft taking part in a Strategic Air Command
exercise, and to distortions of stars and planets caused by
the high temperature. A month later, the police had an
unsolicited letter from Project Blue Book suggesting that
the sightings had been caused by a high altitude Air Force
exercise. When the officers pointed out that this had ended
at 2 am, the Pentagon's response was to re-classify the
sightings as 'unknown'.

A journalist named John G. Fuller became interested in
the sightings, and went himself to investigate. He actually
saw a bright orange-red disc being pursued by a jet fighter.
All this seemed to indicate that the Air Force knew
something about what was going on – a conclusion Fuller
goes to some length to emphasise in his best selling book
Incident at Exeter (1966). Another expert on UFOs, Major
Donald E. Keyhoe, expressed the same kind of doubts in a
book called *Aliens From Space* (1973).

On Tuesday, 9 November, 1965, an enormous blackout
on the east coast of America plunged eighty thousand
square miles into darkness – thirty-six million people – one
fifth of America's population – were affected. Nearly eight
hundred thousand people were trapped for hours in
elevators and underground trains while airline pilots circled
trying to find a way to land at darkened airports. Fortunately, few people seem to have been injured or even
seriously inconvenienced, although nine months later,
statisticians noted a surge in the birth rate which indicated
that most Americans had chosen a predictable alternative to
television.

Two days later, it was announced that the problem had been caused by a break in the power line from Niagara. A check showed that this was untrue. Then the authorities announced that the problem lay at a remote-control sub-station at Clay, New York, where high tension wires above the town are part of a 'super highway' of power from Niagara Falls to New York City. But repair men who drove out to Clay found nothing wrong.

In *Incident at Exeter*, John Fuller reports: 'Something else happened outside Syracuse, however, which was noted briefly in the press, and then immediately dropped without follow-up comment. Weldon Ross, a private pilot and instructor, was approaching Hancock Field at Syracuse for a landing. It was at almost the exact moment of the blackout. As he looked below him, just over the power lines near the Clay sub-station, a huge red ball of brilliant intensity appeared. It was about a hundred feet in diameter, Ross told the New York *Journal-American*. He calculated that the fireball was at the point where the New York Power Authority's two 345,000-volt power-lines at the Clay sub-station pass over New York Central's tracks between Lake Oneida and Hancock Field. With Ross was a student pilot who verified the statement. At precisely the same moment, Robert C. Walsh, Deputy Commissioner for the Federal Aviation Agency in the Syracuse area, reported that he saw the same phenomenon just a few miles south of Hancock Field. A total of five persons reported the sighting. Although the Federal Power Commission immediately said they would investigate, no further word has been given publicly since.'

Major Donald Keyhoe continues the story: 'other pilots and assorted witnesses reported other sightings elsewhere. Two civilians in flight over Pennsylvania shortly before the blackout began witnessed two UFOs flying above them with Air Force jet interceptors in pursuit. Also just before

On the morning of 17 April, 1966, Dale F. Spaur, Deputy Sheriff of Portage County, Ohio, was notified that a UFO had caused a car's engine to stall. He and his assistant drove to the scene, and saw the UFO. As the machine flew away to the east, Spaur drove at top speed after it – sometimes reaching a hundred miles an hour. Forty miles away from the point where he started, Spaur was joined by another police car, driven by Officer Wayne Huston of East Palestine. Huston also saw the UFO. He said it was 'shaped something like an ice-cream cone with a sort of partly melted top.' The chase continued into Pennsylvania, ending in Conway. Officer Frank Panzanella of Conway told them that he had been watching the shining object for about ten minutes. All four then saw the UFO rise straight up into the night sky and disappear.

According to Project Blue Book what these four independent observers had actually seen was the planet Venus.

the blackout began, a UFO was sighted near the Niagara Falls Power Plant. After it was all over, experts investigating the cause of the breakdown traced its origin to the area of the Clay sub-station, but were unable to find anything wrong with the equipment. When the investigators and journalists began to take the hypothesis of UFO intervention seriously, a previously overlooked broken relay in Ontario was announced to be the cause of the disaster. However, later investigation brought out that the supposedly broken relay had in fact never broken. The supposedly infallible billion dollar US-Canadian grid system dissolved in four seconds flat as the network was suddenly and simultaneously drained of power in some sectors while being overloaded in others. The multiple safety controls supposed to be effective in such an emergency did not work at all. They had worked effectively during previous smaller scale emergency situations. In 1968 Congressman William F. Ryan put McDonald on record concerning UFO activity at the time of the great power failure. Doctor McDonald charged the Federal Power Commission with evading the evidence connecting UFOs to the power failure. As Doctor McDonald made this accusation in Congress, it was entered in the Congressional Record.'

McDonald's statements provoked a torrent of abuse and violent criticism from his colleagues, who denounced him as a crank. On 13 June, 1971, McDonald was found dead, shot through the head with a pistol by his side. The official verdict was suicide.

Again, we note the witnesses who saw UFOs being pursued by aeroplanes, with the implication that the Air Force knew beyond all doubt of the real existence of UFOs, and that the announcement in the Condon Report, four years later, that UFOs constituted no threat to national security may well have been guided by a desire to prevent widespread panic.

The case of Frank Edwards, the journalist who wrote best selling books with titles like *Strange People* and *Strange World* has often been cited as someone who was deliberately 'silenced'. In the 1960s, Edwards ran an extremely popular radio show sponsored by the American Federation of Labour. But he became fascinated by the subject of flying saucers, and wrote a book called *Flying Saucers – Serious Business*, on whose fly leaf appeared a warning that stated that flying saucers can be harmful to human beings, warning readers not to attempt to touch a UFO that has landed. It became a best seller, but

Edwards lost his job on the radio station. George Meany, president of the American Federation of Labour, admitted that Edwards had been dropped 'because he talked too much about flying saucers'. Edwards learned later that his mention of flying saucers had irritated the Defence Department who had brought pressure to bear on Meany.

Edwards was not silenced for long – he soon had his own syndicated radio show that dealt almost exclusively with flying saucers. But in June 1967, whilst still in his fifties, Edwards collapsed and died. The news of his death caused consternation at the 1967 Congress of Scientific Ufologists in New York's Hotel Commodore, because it so happened that the day, June 24 was precisely twenty years after Kenneth Arnold had made the first well known UFO sighting near Mount Rainier. Edwards's obituary stated that his death was 'apparently due to a heart attack'.

But whether his death has some genuine sinister connotation, there can be no doubt that he was, in fact, silenced for a while by the US Defence Department.

Was Edwards merely being paranoid in believing that UFOs can be dangerous? Jacques Vallee has argued strongly that this is untrue. In a book called *Confrontations* (1990), he cites many cases in which it seems that human beings have been physically damaged – sometimes killed – by their contact with UFOs. In 1980, Vallee and his wife Janine went to investigate a case that had taken place near Rio de Janeiro in August 1966. An eighteen-year-old boy had found the corpses of two men when he was looking for a lost kite. They were dressed in neat suits and new raincoats, and lying on their backs. There was no blood, no sign of violence at the site. The two corpses were lying peacefully side by side. Next to them were crude metal masks and slips of paper covered with notes. One of these notes contained elementary electrical formulae.

UFOs

The corpses were decomposed and the coroner concluded that death was caused by cardiac arrest – although he did not explain why two men had died of it at the same time. He was able to say that the men had died some time between 16 August and 20 August.

The men were identified as two electronics technicians named Miguel Jose Viana, thirty-four, and Manuel Pereira da Cruz, thirty-two. Both lived in the town of Campos, and specialised in putting up local tv transmitters.

When news of the double death was publicised, a society woman named Gracinda de Souza reported that she had been driving with three of her children on Wednesday, 17 August when they saw an oval object, orange in colour, with a line of fire around its edges 'sending out rays in all directions'. It hovered over the hill where the bodies were found. Soon after this, many witnesses called the police to report that they had seen an orange coloured, egg-shaped object giving off blue rays over the hill.

The metal masks – they were made of lead – naturally gave rise to a suspician that the men were expecting to encounter something that might give off dangerous rays.

Jacques Vallee became interested in the case when a doctor named Olavo Fontes visited him in Chicago in 1967 and handed him a bundle of reports which included an account of the strange deaths. It also mentioned an event that had taken place a few months before the sighting, on 16 March, 1966, when a luminous object, eliptical in shape, was seen at an altitude of a hundred feet not far from the later sightings.

When Vallee and his wife went to Brazil in 1980 to investigate the site of the tragedy, he began to gather information about other people who had been seriously damaged by UFOs.

He learned, for example, of an event that had taken place in 1946, when two men, Prestes Filho and a friend were

returning from a fishing trip near the village of Aracrigua-
ma, and who separated at seven o'clock in the evening. An
hour later, Prestes staggered into his sister's home with a
story of a beam of light that had hit him as he was reaching
his front door. That same evening his condition deteriorated and Vallee learned that 'his flesh literally detached
itself from his bones. It was as if he had been boiled in hot
water for a long time, so that his skin and the underlying
tissue fell.' On route to the hospital, he died. Later, the skin
continued to fall away from his body until his corpse looked
'decomposed'.

The possibility that he was struck by lightning was
discounted when it was revealed that on the evening in
question the sky was perfectly clear.

On 17 August, 1962, in the town of Duas Pontes, Brazil, a
man called Rivalino Mafra noticed two small beings digging
a hole near his house – they ran away as he came closer and
moments later he saw an object shaped like a hat take off
from behind some bushes, surrounded by a red glow.

On 19 August, two days later, Rivalino and his three
sons were awakened by the sound of heavy footsteps and
saw shadows shaped like human beings floating through
the house and voices that threatened them. One of the
sons later testified to the police: 'I saw two balls floating
in mid air side by side, about a foot apart, and three feet
off the ground ... they were big ... one of them was
black, with a kind of irregular antenna-like extension and a
small tail. The other was black and white with the same
outline ... both emitted a humming sound ... I called
my father out of the house ... he walked towards the
object and stopped about two yards away. At that
moment the two big spheres merged into each other.
There was now only one, bigger in size, raising dust from
the ground, and giving off smoke that darkened the sky.
With strange sounds, the large ball crept slowly towards
my father.

I saw him surrounded by yellow smoke; he disappeared inside it. I ran after him into the yellow cloud, which had an acrid smell. I saw nothing, only that yellow mist around me. I yelled for my father but there was no answer. Everything was silent again. Then the yellow smoke dissolved. The spheres were gone. My father was gone . . . I want my father back.'

A local doctor called Pereira had also seen a disc-shaped object on the day of Rivalino's disappearance.

Vallee also reports a case that took place on 5 July, 1969, near the town of Anolaima, Colombia, about 40 miles north west of Bogota. At 8.30 in the evening, two children saw a luminous object 300 yards away. They grabbed a flashlight and sent out signals. It came closer and the children called out the rest of the family, and all thirteen people who lived in the farmhouse watched the light as it flew off and disappeared behind a hill. The father, fifty-four-year-old Arcesio Bermudez took the flashlight and went to investigate. When he came back he was frightened. From a distance of less than twenty feet he had seen a small person inside the top part of the object, which was transparent, while the rest of the craft was dark. He saw this being when he turned on his flashlight. The object then became bright and took off.

Over the next few days his health deteriorated and forty-eight hours after the sighting he felt sick. He was unable to eat, and had dark blue spots on his skin. Seven days later he died. But the doctors who diagnosed gastro-enteritis as the cause of death were not told about the UFO incident, and one of them later commented 'if I had known of his experience I would have performed more tests.'

In one incident described by Vallee, five people died near the town of Parnarama at different times, following close encounters with UFOs. These were all deer-hunters who had climbed into trees at night to wait for their quarry.

Witnesses reported rectangular objects sometimes looking like refrigerators, flying over the treetops and shining a beam towards the earth – local inhabitants came to call them chupas. Rivamar Ferreira was out with his friend Abel Boro on 17 October, 1981, when they saw a light that turned night into day. Abel screamed as the object – looking like a giant spinning truck tyre with lights on it – surrounded his body with a glittering glow. Ferreira ran to Abel's house and returned with his family; they found Abel Boro dead, his body white 'as if drained of blood'.

In another case, a man called Dionizio General was on top of a hill when an object hovered over him and shot a beam at him like 'a big ray of fire'. A witness testified that he seemed to receive a shock and came rolling down the hill. For the next three days he was insane with terror, then died. Vallee also cites cases in which two victims, Raimundo Souza, and a man named Ramon who lived in Panorama, died shortly after similar encounters.

Interviewing local inhabitants of Panorama, Vallee noted that one witness compared the beam to an electric arc, while another said he remembered a very bad smell like an electrical odour (ozone?) and saw a blinding light, with pulsating colours inside. Many other people who reported being exposed to 'chupas' as they were lying in tree hammocks said that, several years later, they still suffered from headaches and general weakness, and had lost their previous vitality.

Jaques Vallee concludes his chapter with a comment: 'many of the injuries described in Brazil . . . are consistent with the effects of high-power pulsed microwaves.' In other words, there is a sense in which the victims were 'cooked' exactly as if they had placed their hands in an unprotected microwave oven.

John Keel remains convinced that the 'visitors from space' have other ways of destroying people. In *Operation Trojan Horse* he tells a strange story.

UFOs

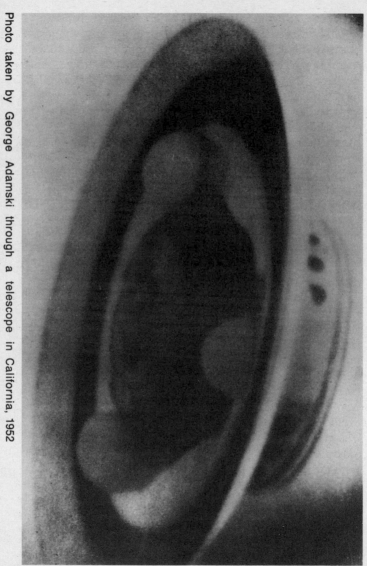

Photo taken by George Adamski through a telescope in California, 1952

In 1959, there appeared a typical 'contactee' book called *My Contact With Flying Saucers* by a man who called himself Dino Craspedon, written originally in Portuguese. The author claims that, in November 1952, he was touring with a friend in the States of Sao Paolo, and that on reaching the top of the Angatuba Range, they saw five flying saucers hovering in the air. He went back to the same spot later and spent three days and nights in the hope of seeing a saucer again. On the last night, he claims that a saucer landed, and he was taken inside it by the captain and introduced to its crew.

In March 1953, there was a knock at Dino Craspedon's door – his name was actually Aladino Felix – and a man who looked like a parson asked if he could speak to Aladino. To Aladino's surprise, it was the captain from a flying saucer. Aladino claims that the captain revealed himself to be a man of tremendous erudition, speaking Greek, Latin and Hebrew, and claiming that he came from a satellite of Jupiter.

The book that followed was basically a dialogue between Aladino and the captain of the spacecraft. It differs from most 'contactee' books in being full of rather precise scientific detail, and even a certain amount of mathematics.

The book failed to cause any sensation at the time, and most people naturally dismissed it as fiction – like the works of George Adamski. However, John Keel seems to feel that the book is genuine. He says: 'a careful reading reveals a thorough knowledge of both theology and science, and many of the ideas and phrases found only in most obscure occult and contactee literature appear here. Among other things, the book also discusses an impending cosmic disaster in lucid almost convincing terms; the same kind of warning that is passed on to every contactee in one way or another.'

Keel goes on to explain that in 1965, Aladino Felix turned up in Brazil claiming to be able to predict the future.

He warned of a disaster about to take place in Rio de Janeiro, and a month later, floods and landslides killed six hundred people. In 1966 he warned that a Russian cosmonaut would die, and in April 1967, Vladimir Komarov became the first man to die in space. In the autumn of 1967 Felix appeared on television in Brazil to soberly discuss the forthcoming assassinations in the United States of Martin Luther King and Senator Robert Kennedy.

When he started predicting an outbreak of bombings and murders in Brazil in 1968 no one was greatly surprised when a wave of terrorist attacks began.

'Police stations and public buildings in Sao Paolo were dynamited. There was a wave of bank robberies, and an armoured payroll train was heisted. The Brazilian police worked overtime and soon rounded up eighteen members of the gang. A twenty-five-year-old policeman named Jesse Morais proved to be the gang's bomb expert. They had blown up Second Army Headquarters, a major newspaper, and even the American Consulate. When the gang members started to sing, it was learned that they planned to assassinate top government officials and eventually take over the entire country of Brazil. Jesse Morais had been promised the job of Police Chief in the new government.

'The leader of this ring was . . . Aladino Felix!

'When he was arrested on 22 August, 1968, the flying saucer prophet declared, "I was sent here as an ambassador to the earth from Venus. My friends from space will come here and free me and avenge my arrest. You can look for tragic consequences to humanity when the flying saucers invade this planet".'

Keel comments: 'once again the classic, *proven* pattern has occurred. Another human being had been engulfed by the ultraterrestrials and led down the road to ruin. There is no clinical psychiatric explanation for these cases. These men (and it has happened to women too) experienced a succession of convincing events with flying saucers and the UTs.

Then they were smothered with promises or ideas which destroyed them.'

If Keel is correct, then the 'space people' themselves seem as anxious to cover-up their activities as the government agencies denounced by Hynek and Vallee.

Chapter Five

THE PSYCHIC
SOLUTION?

The Loch Ness Ghost?

In August 1962, a fishing journalist named Frederick William Holiday — known to his friends as Ted — drove in a light van to the shores of Loch Ness. He had always been fascinated by the mystery of the Loch Ness Monster. That night, as he was sleeping in his tent, he was puzzled to hear the sound of waves crashing on the beach. The night was windless and totally silent, and there was no sound of a boat out on the Loch — in any case navigation is forbidden by night. Whatever was causing the continuous sound of waves must have been fairly large. Two days later, he was up at dawn, standing on a hillside with binoculars in his hand when he had the first sighting of the monster. Something black and glistening and rounded appeared above the surface, projecting about three feet. Then it dived producing an upsurge of water like a diving hippopotamus. Through his binoculars he could make out the shape below the surface — thick in the middle and tapering towards its extremities. Holiday guessed it to be between forty and forty-five feet long.

Three years later, in 1965, he sighted it on two more occasions. After that first sighting, he felt relatively sure that what he'd been watching was simply a giant version of the common garden slug, an ancestor of the squid and octopus. And in 1968, he produced a book called *The Great Orm of Loch Ness*, in which the main argument is that the monster is a variety of giant slug, *Tullimonstrum Gregarium*, a creature looking a little like a submarine with a broad tail, and that these monsters were once altogether more plentiful in the United Kingdom – hence the many legends of dragons. He also adds, almost casually, that the dragon seems to be often regarded as a symbol of evil.

What struck him as so odd was the apparent camera-shyness of the monster. Again and again he heard stories of people who had seen it, but by the time they had raised their camera, or gone to the car to get it, it had vanished. It almost seemed as if the monster was telepathic.

Later in 1968, he heard the report of a monster in a small lough (the Irish version of a loch) near Claddaghduff, in Galway. But when Ted went to Lough Fadda, he was puzzled that it seemed too small to house a monster; a fifteen foot 'pieste' (as the Irish call them) would soon eat all the fish and die of starvation. Yet when he spoke to witnesses, and studied accounts of other sightings in Ireland, it seemed clear that the sightings were genuine; on one occasion, the witnesses were two priests, on another, a middle aged librarian. Such people would hardly be likely to invent a monster-sighting to gain notoriety.

Besides, there are too many stories about lake monsters for them to be invention. In the early nineteenth century, Thomas Croker collected many of them, which he published in a book of Irish legends. He sent this to Sir Walter Scott, who replied that many people near Abbotsford – where he lived – swore to having seen a 'water-bull' emerge from a lake hardly large enough to have held him. An Irish woman who saw one described it as having a head like a horse and a tail like an eel, and called it a horse-eel. But dozens of descriptions make it clear that the Irish lake monsters belong to the same family as the Loch Ness Monster.

Holiday decided to set up nets in a small lake called Lough Nahooin, where a 'water-horse' had been sighted. Something disturbed the nets; but there was no evidence that it was a lake monster. But Ted encountered another odd coincidence. While he was near the lough, he had neuralgic pains in his jaws which made sleep impossible, and they came and went over many days; his companion also suffered from them. Later, reading the *Egyptian Book of the Dead* he came across a description of a 'Worm' of the marshes, and the worm is made to ask the goddess Ea (which signifies 'antelope of the deep') if he can 'drink among the teeth, and . . . devour the blood of the teeth and of their gums.'

Now although he does not say so, I think we may infer — from the number of times he mentions him — that Ted was reading a great deal of Jung at this time and that he was interested in Jung's notion that flying saucers may be some kind of 'projection' of the human mind. It now began to strike him that, whether lake monsters were 'projections' or not, they certainly seemed to belong to some strange realm midway between the physical and the psychological.

Ted had himself seen a number of unidentified flying objects, and was apparently much taken with Jung's theory. If Flying Saucers can be a 'projection' of man's basic craving for 'goodness', then was it not just as conceivable that lake monsters may be a projection of man's religious sense of evil? After all, the dragon was an ancient symbol of wickedness, hence the legend of St George, and if Holiday was correct in his original assumption that dragons, 'worms' and lake monsters are the same thing, then the Loch Ness Monster might be as unreal — objectively speaking — as the Jungian flying saucer . . .

Now he began to toy with the idea that there may be some 'Jungian' connection between the deep realities of the human psyche and the elusive mystery of lake monsters *and* flying saucers. So he embarked on a wide range of study of the literature of the past, in an attempt to trace a connection between UFOs, lake monsters and ancient religious symbols. He turned his attention to archaeology, and was intrigued by the mystery of the barrows. There seemed to be two types of barrow – or burial mound – long barrows and round barrows (also a called disc barrows.) Most of them date from the bronze age. Many barrows contain ritual objects in the shape of discs – presumably sun-discs. Holiday looked at many photographs of disc barrows – for example at Winterbourne Stoke, near Stonehenge – and was struck by their resemblance to certain well-known flying saucer photographs. And in *The Dragon and the Disc* (1973), he boldly proposed the theory that the 'barrow culture' was, in effect, a flying saucer culture: that the builders of these great mounds were imitating objects they had seen in the sky. Holiday notes that many UFO sightings include 'cigar-shaped' objects, and that some people claimed to have seen the smaller 'flying saucers' emerging from the cigar-shaped objects. The long barrows, he suggested, were based on the cigar-shaped UFOs.

There is, of course, a certain danger in constructing theories like these, a danger that can be seen very clearly in the work of Eric von Daniken. Holiday, fortunately, was not prone to the kind of enthusiasm that destroys all critical balance. Like Jacques Vallee, he was moving towards the view that flying saucers may be symbols – or perhaps a better word would be signals; that is to say, that their purpose may be to 'remind' human beings that reality is altogether stranger and more complex than they think. The question of precisely who is making the signals is left open. But in the twelfth chapter of *The Dragon and the Disc*, he admits that 'by 1970 I had rejected the superficial view of monster phenomena – that they are just unknown animals that have somehow escaped the science net – as inadequate.' He goes on to suggest that in the ancient world, the 'disc' may have been worshipped in many places, while the dragon was worshipped by other groups. Such groups today would be called satanists. He points out that Irish churches seem to lack the serpent designs found in so many English churches, and suggests that perhaps this is what is meant by the legend that St Patrick banished the serpents from Ireland — that he destroyed the ancient religion of dragon worship.

In a final chapter, 'An Exercise in Speculation', he makes a heroic effort to pull together all the various threads of the book, but it is well-nigh an impossibility. He speaks about 'other dimensions' and parallel universes, and points out that in many reports of UFOs, the object seemed to come and go, materialising and dematerialising moment by moment. Then he goes on to mention some of the odd phenomena observed in the Warminster area — where many flying saucers had been observed; for example, a couple who were driving home late at night when they saw a corpse lying with its feet in the road; when they stopped the car, it had vanished. But he is obviously not sure how this kind of oddity fits into the general pattern about flying saucers, and about the lines of 'earth force' which have been labelled 'ley lines'. The book seems to fade out on a question-mark which, like the smile of the Cheshire cat, hangs in the air after the rest of it has vanished.

It was some time after this that Ted came into contact with a clergyman named the Rev. Donald Omand, who was an exorcist. Omand had also reached the conclusion that lake monsters are 'evil'. He had seen two small black humps emerge above the surface in Loch Long, in Ross-shire, and assumed that it was simply some curious unknown animal. In the following year he met a Norwegian sailor who told him that he was convinced that there are patches of water that possess 'magnetic' properties which can overcome a man's reason and cause him to jump overboard. Omand accepted his invitation to go and look at the 'eeriest

The Loch Ness Monster

waterway in Norway', known as the Fjord of the Trolls. As the small boat entered the fjord, Omand began to experience a strange feeling of apprehension, and as the boat reached the end of the fjord, it became an atmosphere of menace. The boat then turned and made its way back. Suddenly the water ahead of them 'boiled', and two humps rose above the surface. At close quarters, the monster seemed far larger that the one in Loch Long, and Omand was terrified that it would overturn the small boat. But the Norwegian told him not to worry – 'It won't hurt us – they never do', and the creature veered just before it reached the boat and dived. When Omand suggested following it, the Norwegian shook his head. 'Sufficient unto the day is the evil thereof. And I *mean* evil.' 'Why evil?' asked Omand, 'it did us no harm.' 'They don't do physical harm. They want to convince anyone who sees them that they are harmless. The evil they do is to men's characters.' And he told Omand that he thought they were somehow connected with the biblical serpent.

In 1972, Omand attended a psychiatric conference in Sweden, and was intrigued when an eminent psychiatrist read a paper on the monster of Lake Storsjon, in which he said that he was convinced that such monsters had a malevolent effect on human beings – on those who hunted it and on those who saw it regularly. He thought their influence could produce domestic tragedies and moral degeneration. He had investigated cases in Scotland and Ireland, and claimed that 'the same pattern of domestic tragedy had emerged'. It was now that Omand began to formulate his theory that lake monsters were not solid entities, but a 'projection into our day and age' of something from the prehistoric past.

A newspaper story led Ted Holiday to write to Omand, and the result was a curious episode in which the two of them went out on to Loch Ness and performed a ceremony of exorcism. It left them both oddly exhausted. Two days later, Holiday went to visit some friends, the Careys, and mentioned that he meant to go and examine the place in nearby woods where a Swedish journalist had seen a grounded UFO. Mrs Carey and her husband had also seen an orange-coloured ball of light over Loch Ness, and Mrs Carey warned Ted against going to the place where the grounded UFO had been seen. The journalist, Jan-Ove Sundberg claimed to have been harrassed by 'men in black' after he had returned to Sweden, and had suffered a nervous breakdown. Holiday tells how, as Mrs Carey was giving him this advice, there was a rushing sound like a tornado outside the window, and a series of violent thuds; Ted saw a pyramid of blackish smoke whirling outside. Mrs Carey saw a beam of white light which focussed on Ted's forehead. Basil Carey, who was standing with his back to the window pouring a drink, heard nothing and saw nothing. The garden proved to be empty and perfectly normal.

The next morning, as he walked out of the house, Ted saw a 'man in black' who appeared to be waiting for him – the man was dressed in black leather, with goggles and a helmet. Ted walked up to him, and turned his eyes away for about ten seconds; in that time, the man vanished. One year later, near the same spot, Ted had his first heart attack – he describes looking over the side of the stretcher and seeing that they'd just passed over the spot where he'd seen the man in black. Five years later, he died of another heart attack.

Holiday admitted that his viewpoint had changed completely between the mid 1960s and the mid 1970s,, and he tried to explain this in his final book *The Goblin Universe*. It was an attempt to sketch this 'new look' universe in which he found himself. Tom Lethbridge – whom we have already met – once described how he had been walking on the arctic ice when it collapsed, and he found himself floundering in freezing water; he compares this to his sensations when he began investigating the strange world of dowsing. Ted Holiday had also started off with a perfectly sensible and scientific curiosity about the Loch Ness Monster – and to a lesser extent, UFOs. And, little by little, he was forced to admit that his common sense explanations failed to fit the facts. For a man of his pragmatic temperament, it must have cost a great deal of mental struggle to associate himself with Donald Omand in exorcising Loch Ness. Unfortunately, Holiday decided to suppress the *The Goblin Universe*, because some of the underwater photographs of the Loch Ness Monster taken in the 1970s made him begin to wonder whether it was simply some unknown animal. Fortunately, he and I had been in correspondence for some years, and I had a copy of the typescript of the book at the time Ted died. I was able to persuade an American publisher (Llewellyn) to bring it out, and the royalties went to Ted's mother.

I can understand why he began to experience doubts about publishing it. What the book shows very clearly is how someone who starts off with a sensible and scientific attitude can be drawn in more and more deeply until finally he experiences a sense of total bewilderment, and realises that the conclusions he is reaching definitely place him within the 'lunatic fringe'. And yet every one of these conclusions seems completely logical. It was worth getting *The Goblin Universe* into print merely as a record of this bewildering journey which has been taken by so many of those who became interested in UFOs.

Puharich and Geller

The late Andriya Puharich, who died in 1995, followed this same bewildering and confusing path from the normal to the paranormal.

It was as a psychologist that Puharich studied a young Dutch sculptor named Harry Stone who, when examining

In 1965, there were two UFO sightings at a point called Colloway Clump on the Warminster-Westbury Road in Wiltshire. And in a field near the bend in the road, circular depressions were found in the crops which were labelled 'UFO nests'.

In the 1980s, a Wiltshire farmer named John Scull found his oats crushed to the ground in three separate circles not far from Colloway Clump. The circles were surrounded by undamaged oats and no paths through the corn suggested intruders.

As the decade progressed, there were an increasing number of these 'crop circles'. Many of the reports came from southern England, but there were others from Australia, New Zealand, Argentina, Brazil, South Africa, Mexico, America, Canada, France, Spain, Switzerland, Austria, Germany, Sweden, Russia and even Japan. In many cases, the crop circles were found in fields near UFO sightings.

Scientific investigators suggested that the circles were created by some kind of natural whirlwind, at which point, circles began to appear in more complex forms – sometimes like a dumb bell, sometimes rather like a key, sometimes like a Celtic cross. Another crop pattern seemed to represent a kind of chemical retort with a long neck, with four rectangles neatly spaced on either side of it.

Witnesses came forward who had seen grass laid out flat as a curious humming sound vibrated through the air. One witness who rushed forward into the circle said that he seemed to be caught up in a whirlwind. A moment later, everything was still.

In 1990, John Michell made the suggestion that the meaning of the crop circles 'is to be found in the way people are affected by them'. He seemed to feel that crop circles could be some kind of 'teaching experience' designed to awaken peoples' minds to wider possibilities.

In 1991, two men called Douglas Bower and David Chorley admitted that since 1978 they had faked hundreds of crop circles in the south of England, and demonstrated how they did it using wooden boards and lengths of twine. But they never claimed to have made any of the earlier crop circles, and investigators pointed out that, as in an earlier hoax perpetrated by the *Daily Mirror*, the Chorley-Bower crop circles were visibly amateurish.

---

an ancient Egyptian pendant, fell into a trance and began drawing hieroglyphics on a sheet of paper; he also began to speak about his upbringing in ancient Egypt. An expert verified that the hieroglyphics were genuine, and belonged to the period of the Pharaoh Snefru. In his book *The Sacred Mushroom*, Puharich describes the sessions in which he placed Stone under hypnosis, and of how Stone described a cult of the 'Sacred Mushroom' which has now been forgotten.

Next, Puharich began a series of experiments in telepathy with well-known psychics like Peter Hurkos and Eileen Garrett. *Beyond Telepathy* (1962) quickly became a classic in its field.

It was at this point that Puharich came close to destroying his career with an astonishing book called *Uri: A Journal of the Mystery of Uri Geller* (1974). This is a straightforward narrative of Puharich's three-year investigation of Geller; yet it ends by producing total confusion and bewilderment.

The book begins in 1952, long before the two men met; it tells how, when Puharich was studying a Hindu psychic named Dr Vinod, the latter began to speak in a strange voice with a perfect English accent. The voice explained that it was a member of the 'Nine Principles and Forces', superhuman intelligences whose purpose is to aid human evolution.

Three years later, travelling in Mexico, Puharich met an American doctor and his wife, who also passed on lengthy messages from 'space intelligences'; the remarkable thing was that these messages were a continuation of the communications that had come through Dr Vinod. It began to look as if 'the Nine' might really exist.

In 1963, Puharich made the acquaintance of the Brazilian 'psychic surgeon' Arigo, who performed his operations with a kitchen knife which he wiped on his shirt after dealing with each case. Arigo believed he was possessed by the spirit of a dead German surgeon; according to his biographer, he had an unbroken record of successes over many years. Puharich was informed of Arigo's death in a car crash, in January 1971; he afterwards became convinced that he must have received the telephone message a quarter of an hour *before* Arigo died.

All this was a prelude to Puharich's meeting with the famous 'metal bender' Uri Geller, which occurred in a Jaffa discotheque in August 1971 – two years before Geller achieved sudden fame through an appearance on BBC television. Geller's feats of telepathy and precognition impressed Puharich; and if the book was restricted to describing these feats, it would undoubtedly impress most open-minded readers. But at this point, the 'extra-terrestrials' re-enter the story, and it turns into a chronicle of marvels and improbabilites. Placed in a trance, Geller described how, at the age of three, he had fallen asleep in a garden opposite his home, and awakened to see a huge, shining figure standing over him and a bright, bowl-shaped object floating in the sky overhead. And while Geller was still hynotised, a mechanical voice began to speak from the air above his head, explaining that 'they' (the 'space intelligences') had found Geller in the garden, and had been 'programming' him ever since. Puharich, the voice said, had been selected to take care of Uri. The world was in danger of plunging into war, because Egypt was planning to attack Israel, and somehow Geller and Puharich had been given the task of averting the conflict.

When Geller recovered from the trance, he grabbed the cassette on which Puharich had been recording the proceedings, and Puharich swears he saw it vanish in Geller's hand. It was never recovered. This was to be a recurring pattern whenever 'the Nine' communicated; they would either cause the tape to vanish, or wipe the recordings from it.

It would serve no purpose to detail the marvels that fill the rest of the book. Objects are always disappearing and then reappearing. UFOs are sighted. The car engine stops and starts again for no reason. Puharich's camera bag is miraculously 'teleported' three thousand miles from New York to Tel Aviv. The war between Egypt and Israel is somehow averted, although without Puharich's intervention. This relentless succession of miracles leaves the reader bewildered and exhausted, until curiosity finally turns to a kind of punch-drunk indifference.

Understandably, the book did Geller no good at all with the general public. Instead of making converts, it turned believers into sceptics. There was something slightly comic in the assertion that Geller was the ambassador of super-human intelligences, and that the proof lay in his ability to bend spoons. It seemed that Puharich was simply pitching Geller's claim too high, and his obvious sincerity did nothing to improve the situation. The opposition could be divided into two factions: those who believed that Geller and Puharich were trying to hoodwink the rest of the world, and those who thought Geller had hoodwinked Puharich. Not long after the book's publication, Geller and Puharich decided to go their separate ways.

At this point, one might be forgiven for assuming that the more extreme phenomena would cease. In fact – as Stuart Holroyd has revealed in a book called *Prelude to the Landing on Planet Earth* – 'the Nine' apparently continued to manifest themselves as bewilderingly as ever. His story begins in 1974, when Puharich went to Florida to investigate a half-Indian psychic healer, Bobby Horne (this is not his real name). In a hypnotic trance, Horne began to speak in a strange voice, and introduced himself as an extra-terrestrial intelligence named Ancore. His purpose, he said, was to inform the human race that the space intelligences would be arriving on earth *en masse* during the next year or so, and to try to prepare mankind for that traumatic event. Since the voices that had spoken through Geller had made the same claim, Puharich was understandably impressed.

Further tests took place at Ossining, New York. Others present were the author Lyall Watson, an Englishman named Sir John Whitmore, and Phyllis Schlemmer, a 'psychic' who had introduced Puharich to Bobby Horne. They were told, through 'Ancore', that Bobby Horne had been specially prepared for his healing tasks by having invisible wires inserted into his neck by the space intelligences. Equally startling information came through an 'extra-terrestrial' called Tom, who spoke through Phyllis Schlemmer, and who offered a potted history of the human race. The first civilisation was founded 32,000 years ago, in the Tarim Basin of China, by beings from space. At this time, according to 'Tom', there were 'three cultures, three divisions, from three areas of the universe'. A more advanced civilisation was begun, then destroyed through a massacre.

This was to be the pattern of the communications for some time to come. 'Ancore' spoke (through Bobby Horne) about the projected landing of UFOs, and how the space intelligences were trying to devise methods of interfering with television transmissions, so as to be able to speak directly to mankind. And Tom, speaking through Phyllis Schlemmer, went into considerable detail about earlier civilisations, and the purpose of man on earth. The earth, says Tom, is unique in the universe; every soul must pass through it sooner or later. 'It is the love of this planet that generates the energy that becomes God.' The earth is a kind of school, disigned to teach the balance between the spiritual and the physical. But mankind has become too negative, and has created a force of active evil. It has become a kind of bottleneck in the universe, blocking its evolution. Unless man evolves a new type of consciousness, or unless he receives help from outside, the earth will enter a new ice age within two centuries, due to pollution of the atmosphere.

Eventually, Bobby Horne began to find all this talk about space intelligences too oppressive, and went back to his wife in Florida. Lyall Watson also declined to become a permanent part of the team, on the grounds that he had to get back to writing books. This left Puharich, Phyllis Schlemmer and Sir John Whitmore, whose fortune was to finance some of the hectic activity of the next two years.

The remainder of Holroyd's long book is too confusing to attempt a detailed summary. What happened, basically, was that Puharich, Whitmore and Phyllis Schlemmer spent a great deal of time rushing around the world – often suspected of being spies – and sitting in hotel rooms listening to instructions from 'Tom' and praying for world peace. Periodically, Tom congratulated them, and explained that they had just averted some international catastrophe, such as the assassination of the Palestinian leader Yasser Arafat. The book ends, as all good books should, with a dramatic climax in which the three musketeers avert a Middle Eastern war by driving around Israel holding meditation sessions and otherwise 'diffusing a vapour trail of love and peace'. At the end of this agitated pilgrimage, 'Tom' assures them that their efforts have been successful and that the Middle East will cease to be a flashpoint for some time to come. With a sound sense of literary structure, he even advises Puharich to use these events as the climax of the book he intends to write. (In fact, Puharich passed on the job to Stuart Holroyd.) We are told in a postscript that equally weird things have been taking place since the successful peace mission in March 1975, but that these must wait for a future instalment.

In the bibliography of *Prelude to the Landing on Planet Earth*, Holroyd cites a nineteenth-century classic of psychical investigation, *From India to the Planet Mars*, by Theodore Flournoy, and readers of Holroyd may find the parallel instructive. In 1894, Flournoy, a well-known psychologist, investigated the mediumship of an attractive girl named Catherine Muller (whom he called Heléne Smith). He was soon convinced of the genuineness of her powers; she was able to tell him about events that occurred in his family before he was born. In later seances, Catherine went into deeper trances, and began to describe her 'past incarnations' – as the wife of a Hindu prince of the fifteenth century, as Marie Antoinette, and as an observer of life on Mars. Flournoy remains sceptical. The Hindu incarnation is often convincing; she seemed to have considerable knowledge of the language and customs of fifteenth-century India, and even named a prince, Sivrouka Nakaya, who was later found to have been a historical personage. By contrast, the descriptions of Mars are absurd, with yellow sky, red hills, bug-eyed monsters, and buildings that look just like human beings; their language, as transribed by her, is suspiciously like French.

If any charitable spiritualists felt inclined to give Catherine the benefit of the doubt, their justification for doing so vanished in September 1976, when the Viking landing on Mars revealed the planet to be an arid desert with no sign of life – even minute organisms.

Yet Catherine Muller cannot be dismissed as a fraud, even of the unconscious variety. Her knowledge of Flournoy's past showed that she possessed genuine powers of telepathy. While she was in trance, Flournoy witnessed 'apports' of Chinese shells and coins, and even roses and violets in midwinter. Paranormal forces undoubtedly were at work, but Flournoy declined to allow this to persuade him that Catherine had really been a Hindu princess or had visited Mars.

Flournoy would certainly have been equally sceptical about the narrative in *Prelude to a Landing on Planet Earth*. He would see no reason for rejecting the explanation that he applied to the mediumship of 'Helene Smith': that the answers should be sought in the unconscious minds of the participants. And it must be admitted that Helene's identification of herself with a Hindu princess and Marie Antoinette is, if anything, rather more believable that 'Tom's' revelation that Puharich had once been the god Horus (and later, Pythagoras), while Whitmore had been Thoth and Phyllis Schlemmer Isis . . .

Still, in all fairness, one has to admit that anyone who experienced the events described in *The Sacred Mushroom*, *Uri* and *Prelude to the Landing on Planet Earth* would end up convinced of the existence of space intelligences. If the whole thing is some kind of trick of the unconscious, how does it work? And *whose* unconscious? My own conviction, formed at the time when I was studying Geller at close quarters, was that Puharich himself is the key to the enigma. Uri's powers of telepathy and metal bending struck me as

Israeli psychic Uri Geller

remarkable, and almost certainly genuine; but I never witnessed anything as spectacular as the events that occur on every other page of Puharich's book. My suspicion, quite simply, was that Puharich is himself a gifted 'psychic', and that when he and Geller met, the combination of their subconscious powers, a kind of mutual interaction and prompting, was explosive. Since Puharich was already convinced of the existence of the Nine, it was logical — and almost inevitable — that Geller's trance messages should come from these non-human intelligences. In short, Geller and Puharich somehow united to form a kind of firework display of poltergeist effects. The main question in my mind was simply whether Puharich aided and abetted these effects through wishful thinking and general dottiness.

When I finally met Puharich, and his friend Mrs Joyce Petchek, in June 1976, it was almost an anti-climax. Throughout the whole of a long evening, he neither did nor said anything to suggest mental unbalance, or even the slightest eccentricity. He was a short, grey-haired man with a bushy moustache and rather vague manner. Although in his mid-fifties, he had the kind of innocence and enthusiasm that I associated with American students. He was casual, good-natured and unpretentious. When I explained my theory that he was himself a psychic, and had been partly responsible for the Geller effects, he brooded in it for a few seconds, then said: 'You could be right, but I'm inclined to doubt it.'

It soon became clear that Puharich had had so many strange experiences that he had come almost to take them for granted. He would spend ten minutes describing with great precision a laboratory experiment in which he had tested Peter Hurkos, then tell me of some utterly weird event involving Geller that sounded like science fiction. He told me, for example, of the teleportation of a unique chunk of stone from Ossining to the hotel bedroom of a couple who were making love more than a hundred miles away. A figure identical with Geller knocked on their door and handed them the stone; and afterwards, the stone was there to prove it. But at the time, Geller was in Ossining with Puharich, and knew nothing about it. Puharich told me he had deliberately left many such stories out of his book because it was already overloaded with unbelievable stories.

Joyce Petschek told me an equally strange story. She had been driving from Oxford to London in an attempt to catch a plane, but realised that her chances were minimal; she should have set out at least half an hour earlier. Then, quite suddenly, she found herself close to London, with plenty of time to spare. What had happened, she thinks, is that the car dematerialised at a certain point and simply reappeared fifty miles further on. Both she and a friend who was in the car thought they knew just where it had happened, and where they had 'reappeared'. I should add that Mrs Petschek struck me as being as sane and normal as Puharich, and I had no suspicion that I was witnessing a *folie à deux*. Marvels like this occasionally dropped into the conversation, but always in a rather casual way; clearly, they both accepted them in the way that I had come to accept dowsing for water.

Puharich obviously found my theorising about subconscious poltergeist activity unnecessary. He had long ago reached the conclusion that the Nine are a reality, and that our earth has been observed by space men for thousands of years. He believed that the earth has reached a point in its history where the Nine feel that slightly more intervention is necessary. But public miracles, like a mass landing of UFOs, are probably undesirable. Human beings have to evolve and learn to use their freedom. Too much 'help' from outside would be disastrous because it would make us lazy and dependent, like some primitive tribe suddenly invaded by twentieth-century technology. Instead, Puharich believed, the extra-terrestrials are concentrating on individuals, particularly children, so that the race is changed from within. He claimed he had studied a large number of children of astonishing psychic gifts, not simply the ability to bend spoons, like the protegés of Professor John Taylor, but telepathy and other unusual powers. The great mathematical prodigies of the past, he thought, are a foreshadowing of what is to come.

I found all this convincing, up to a point. Nothing was more obvious than that Puharich and Joyce Petschek were totally sincere in everything that they said. Does this mean that I can accept the existence of the Nine? Obviously not. It is not simply a question of whether I can accept Puharich, Sir John Whitmore and Phyllis Schlemmer as honest, but whether there is now sufficient evidence to convince *any* logical person of the real existence of space beings.

The fact that so many of the 'space intelligences' make contact through 'mediums' suggests that we may be dealing with the same problem that arose in the mid 19th century with the birth of 'Spiritualism'. In 1848, mysterious rappings in the house of the Fox family in Hydesville, New York, led to a nationwide interest in the subject of spirits. The rappings always took place in the presence of the two daughters of the family — aged twelve and fourteen — and were probably some kind of poltergeist activity. But other 'mediums' went into trances and were apparently able to communicate with the spirits of the dead; they were usually taken over by a 'guide' who claimed to come from the 'other world'. The Society for Psychical Research was set up to investigate the phenomena scientifically, and eminent invistigators — like Professor Earnest Bozzano, Professor Charles Richet, F.W.H. Myers — attempted to construct theories that would serve as a foundation for 'psychic science'. None of them came evem remotely near to succeeding. Many mediums proved to be fraudulent; but so many were obviously genuine that the Society for Psychical Research soon became convinced that 'the paranormal' *cannot* be dismissed as a delusion. In fact, some of their investigations were so successful that many came to believe that the final truth about the supernatural would be known by the end of the 19th century, and that ghosts would be as fully understood as electricity and magnetism.

Yet now, more than a hundred years later, we know that such hopes were illusory. Psychical researchers still agree that most of the phenomena are *real*. But they are as far away as ever from an explanation. All of which points to the possibility that the same may prove to apply to the mystery of flying saucers.

Chapter Six

ALIENS AMONG US?

T he latest chapter of the UFO saga is in some ways the most remarkable so far.

It began in the late 1970s, when a New York painter and sculptor called Budd Hopkins became increasingly interested in the phenomenon that we have already encountered many times in this book – 'Missing Time'. We have seen how Betty and Barney Hill suddenly realised that several hours were missing out of a drive back home from Canada, and how, under hypnosis, they remembered being taken on board a space craft. In other words, they had been unwilling 'abductees'.

The psychologist who dealt with the case was inclined to think that it was some kind of hallucination. But since then, dozens – in fact hundreds – of similar cases have thrown some doubt on this simplistic explanation. They suggest that, whatever else they might be, the experiences of 'abductees' are not pure self-delusion.

Oddly enough, Budd Hopkins was among those who felt that Betty and Barney Hill were unconscious self deceivers. Although he had himself had a daylight UFO sighting in 1964, he simply found himself unable to accept the idea of alien abduction. 'Using Justice Frankfurter's distinction, it was not that I thought the Hills were lying, it was just that I could not believe them.' Many psychiatrists believe that the Hills had somehow created the fantasy of being abducted while they were under hypnosis, and then come to accept it as real.

Yet, little by little, his investigation of UFO sightings led him to accept the possibility of alien abduction. In 1981, together with UFO researcher Ted Bloecher and psychologist Doctor Aphrodite Clamar, he wrote the book *Missing Time*, in which he speculated that many people – perhaps thousands – may have had UFO abduction experiences and yet consciously remembered nothing about them. 'The pattern of evidence we had uncovered suggests that a kind of "enforced" amnesia can efficiently erase from conscious memory all but the very slightest recollection of such experiences.'

'In one of the seven similar cases we investigated, "Steven Kilburn" described nothing more than a deep-seated fear of a certain stretch of highway and his "feeling" that something had happened to him there that possibly involved a UFO. Unlike Betty and Barney Hill he did not recall sighting a UFO, he was not aware of any missing time, or even of seeing anything unusual. But after investigating his case with the help of Ted Bloecher, two psychologists and a polygraph operator, I came to the conclusion that his sketchy, though emotion-loaded, initial recollections did in fact conceal a full-blown UFO abduction experience. Under hypnosis Steve relived a traumatic encounter very similar in its details to the Hill case.'

Budd Hopkins reached a startling conclusion. 'It appears that most UFO abductees have had more than one such experience, their first abduction generally occurring in childhood around the age of six or seven. Often they are picked up and examined several times after that, though these later encounters are rarely reported past the age of forty or so. An analogy which immediately springs to mind is the human study of endangered animals, in which zoologists tranquilise and tag or implant transmitters in sample animals to trace their subsequent wanderings. I presented evidence in my book indicating a similar interest by UFO "occupants" in certain human beings who are apparently treated like experimental subjects requiring re-examination at intervals across the years. And as we shall see, there is evidence that these human subjects have also been somehow tagged.'

'A third point dealt with the issue of the still-visible scars which apparently resulted from the UFO occupants systematic, quasi-medical examinations of three people when they were first abducted as children. In the illustration section I reproduced three photographs of these small, straight scars as they currently appeared, respectively, on the back of the calf, above the knee, and on the hip of the three different abductees. (By profession they are a corporation lawyer, a micro-biologist and a news media employee.) As in the Hill case, hypnosis was used to break the memory blocks and to illicit descriptions of the "surgical" procedures which caused the cuts, as well as detailed recollections of the occupants' physical appearance and of the interiors of the UFOs themselves. Though we do not have any indication of the purpose of these incisions, their physical character suggests a cell-sampling operation of some kind. Over the past five years I have encountered twenty-seven more abductees who bear similarly acquired scars, although a number of these marks are of a different type. Instead of a short, straight cut, seven are circular, shallow depressions — scoop marks, one might say — about a quarter to one half inch in diameter.'

As a result of reading *Missing Time*, a woman that Hopkins calls Kathie Davis wrote to him via his publisher.

When Hopkins opened her letter, he found fifteen or so colour photographs. 'I recognised immediately a familiar image from a UFO "landing trace" investigations — a circular area of ground in which all the grass appears to be dead, as if it has been subject to heat or some other form of radiation.'

The experience of Kathie Davis was like that of many other people who have encountered UFOs. She described how, in July 1983, she was about to go out one evening to a neighbour's house when she noticed that the pool house door was open and a light was on. As she had closed it earlier, she mentioned this to her mother before she left. Neither of them was unduly alarmed. Checking again just before she went out, she discovered that the light was now off, the pool house door closed, but the garage door was open – it was always kept shut.

From the neighbour's house, she called her mother and discovered that her mother had seen a 'big light' by the pool house, and that it had moved to a bird feeder on the lawn and grown to about two feet in diameter. She described it as being like a spotlight trained on the bird feeder. Kathie Davis went home, and searched the property. All she found was her dog hiding under a car. The neighbour and her daughter later came back with her and they went swimming. 'Right after that night our yard was burned, by what we don't know. Nothing will grow there now, no matter how much water we give it, and wild animals won't go on it. . . . birds will no longer go near the bird feeder either, and we have always had tons of birds every day, especially rare birds.'

The first thing that struck Hopkins was that the 'burning' of the grass indicated that some kind of landing had taken place, even though neither Kathie nor her mother could remember anything about it.

The photographs showed a large circle, about eight feet in diameter, on the lawn in which all the grass had turned brown. Extending from this circle was a forty-nine foot path which ran nearly perfectly straight and was about three feet in width. The grass on this path was also dead.

Kathie Davis went on to tell him about her sister Laura, a 'realist, very level-headed and not much imagination', who was passing a church when she felt compelled to pull into the parking lot at the back. There she looked up, and saw something silver hovering over the lot, at about the height of a telephone pole, with red, green and white lights flickering on and off. 'All she remembers now is she reached over to turn down her radio to see if it made noise, and then the next thing she remembers is it's dark out and she looks up and this thing is gone and she's driving down the street.'

Kathie Davis described another of her sister's curious experiences. Ten years after the car park experience, she went to a hypnotist to try to lose weight, but it seemed to have the opposite effect on her. In the night after the hypnosis, she woke up and found that she was deaf and dumb. Her husband had to take her to hospital, where she was given tranquilisers. It took some time to improve. Moreover, far from wanting to eat less, she found that eating made her feel much better. When she called the hypnotist to ask him why this should be so, the sound of his voice caused her to feel so violent that she wanted to kill him. Laura was left, with one strong thought: 'that by the year 2000 the world would be totally different than we know it, but it would be only for the young and strong.'

Kathie ended her letter by commenting that both she and her mother had similar scars on their right legs. 'I don't remember when I got mine, but it seems like I had it all my life . . . At first I only had one scar but now I have two, on the same leg.'

Budd Hopkins was naturally intrigued. Laura's experience with a hypnotist suggested that the hypnosis had somehow reawakened the abduction experience that (Hopkins guessed) had taken place in the church car park.

In a telephone conversation Kathie told Hopkins of a disturbing dream she had had shortly after her marriage at the age of nineteen. She was facing two strange, grey-faced creatures who stood by her bed. One of them was holding a small black box with a gleaming red light on it. The two moved forward in total unison, and one of them handed her the box. The creatures, she said, had large heads and almost grey skin, and their eyes were 'pitch black in colour, liquid-like, shimmering in the dim light'.

The 'creature' then told her that at some time in the future, she would see the box again, and then remember it and 'you'll know how to use it'. The dream, she said, seemed 'utterly real'.

Hopkins asked her if she had ever actually *seen* a UFO, and she then described how, as a teenager, she had been driving with two girlfriends in a car when they saw a flashing light in the sky. Somebody said 'It's a UFO', and then, as it came closer, 'we all got a creepy feeling.' They stopped the car to look at it. Kathie could not remember what happened then, so Hopkins asked her if she would call on her friend, Dorothy, and ask her what *she* remembered of the experience. Kathie was surprised when Dorothy remembers even more than she did. Dorothy recalled stopping the car and getting out to look at a light on the ground. Kathie had no memory of getting out of the car. But when she woke up the next morning, she realised that she had arrived home around dawn, and that several hours of the night seemed to be missing.

When he asked Kathie to look more closely at the circular mark on her lawn, Kathie discovered, about two feet beyond the edge of the circle, four small holes, about three inches deep, which could have been made by some sort of landing gear.

Later, Hopkins was to travel to Kathie's home at Copley Woods, near Indianapolis, and interview not only Kathie's mother, but the friend with whom she had spent the evening sewing, Dee Anne, and her eleven-year-old daughter Tammy. Both Dee Anne and Tammy seem to have shared some strange experience that night. Tammy describes feeling nauseated when she went into the pump-house to change into her costume. Dee Anne said that from

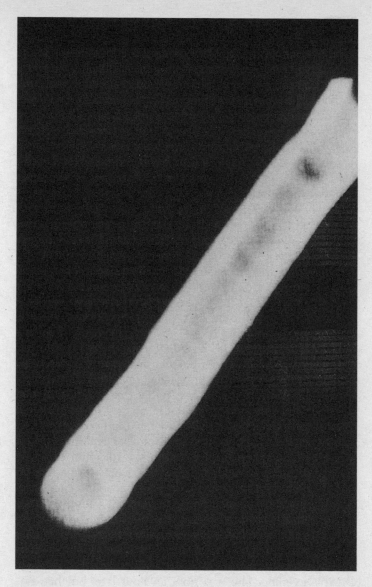

Police patrol photo of UFO in Sicily, 1978

the moment she arrived in Kathie's back yard she felt uneasy, 'like somebody's watching us.' Kathie then described how, as they were swimming in the pool, all three of them suddenly felt freezing cold, although the temperature of the air around them was about 80 degrees. Kathie's eyes began to hurt, and things began to look oddly hazy. Also, all began to feel sick at the same time. For some reason, they decided that they ought to eat, and drove to a nearby fast food resterant, but when they arrived felt so sick that they decided to go straight home.

Neighbours of Kathie Davis – whom Hopkins calls Joyce and Bernie Lloyd – also realised that something odd was going on. Joyce had seen a sudden flash from the direction of Kathie's back yard, followed by a low vibrating sound which caused the house to shake and the chandelier to swing. As the noise increased, the television picture turned red and the lights in the house dimmed and flickered. The sound stopped, and Joyce found herself wondering if she'd been through an earthquake.

Bernie Lloyd described how he came home shortly after all this, and found his wife deeply upset.

Later, Hopkins was to interview Joyce Lloyd, and to discover that she was apparently another abductee. Like so many of them, she had a scar on her leg similar to those on the legs of Kathie and her mother. She could only tell Hopkins that it dated from her childhood, but that its origin was unknown. Then she told him of how, when she was driving home in 1981 from a visit to her mother's, she suddenly found herself becoming confused and disoriented. She pulled off the road, and then was unable to remember anything more until she arrived home to find her phone ringing. It was her mother, who always rang her home after she had been there visiting, just to check that she had arrived home safely. On this evening, she was now an hour late, but had no idea why.

She had also had a strange experience in the summer of 1984. She had awakened in the middle of the night to find herself upside down in bed, with her feet — which were wet — on her pillow. She was wearing shorts and a tee shirt, which were also damp. She had no recollection of going to bed. But she could remember a dream just before she woke up, in which she had been lying in a field, and had seen a light rising into the sky from the edge of the field. She thought she had seen some kind of 'car' in the field, but later said that it was much bigger than a car.

Kathie herself was understandably nervous about these experiences, and wondered what would happen next. Hopkins soothingly reassured her — telling her that UFO experiences generally stopped when investigators like himself began to look into them. Unfortunately, he proved to be wrong. Kathie was due to travel to New York to see him on 13 October, 1983, but ten days before this, she had been lying in bed when she heard her name called quite clearly. She felt it was inside her head rather than outside. She immediately rushed to the phone — in the early hours of the morning — and rang a friend of Budd Hopkins called Sue, who had agreed to be 'on call' in case anything happened.

After this, she awoke her mother, who advised her to take some aspirin and try to get to sleep. Kathie picked up her three-year-old son Tommy, and carried him into her bedroom. As she sat watching the television, she found herself becoming increasingly drowsy, and fell asleep.

Some time later, she was awakened by her mother, who thought that she had heard someone call her name. Kathie said she had been asleep. At that moment, they heard a humming noise from outside the house, rather like a truck with its engine running. Her mother could see nothing out of the window, and finally, they all went back to sleep.

But in the morning, Kathie felt completely exhausted, and had a curious stiffness in her arms, shoulders and neck, 'as if she'd spent the night lifting weights.' Her mother had the same symptoms. When Kathie looked at the bedclothes, she found there were tiny bloodstains on the sheet close to the place where her neck would have rested. There were also stains where her lower back would have rested.

The New York trip went ahead as planned, with Kathie sleeping on a spare bed in Hopkins' studio. She told him that she had suffered various health problems ever since she was very young. She had begun to menstruate at the age of seven, and by the age of ten had high blood pressure. At fourteen, her gall bladder was removed. She suffered from hepatitis and almost died of pneumonia. She had her appendix removed, and once spent two weeks in traction because two vertebrae in her back had somehow fused. The odd thing was that these were extra vertebrae which normal people do not have. In 1983 she had an asthmatic attack. Not long before the experience that led her to write to Hopkins, her heartbeat became so irregular that she needed medical attention.

Hopkins suspected that this long list of illnesses might be connected with some psychological tension due to an abduction experience when she was very young.

When Kathie was fourteen, a small bump appeared on the front of her shin, and she found that she could move it around with her fingers. When she went into hospital for the gall bladder operation, the doctor said he would remove it while she was under the anaesthetic. When she woke up, he showed her a small, bone-like object, and told how, when he sliced into her skin with his scalpel, this had shot straight up several feet into the air, hitting the metal reflector of the surgical lamp with a ping. Unfortunately, Kathie had not kept this cyst.

But Kathie had had an even stranger and more ominous experience. As a teenager, she had been sexually experimental. In 1977, when she was eighteen, she met the man who was to become her husband. Early the following year, she realised that she was pregnant. Medical tests confirmed the pregnancy. They decided to move the wedding forward a few months. Then, one morning in March, she woke up finding herself menstruating normally. A visit to the doctor confirmed the fact that she was no longer pregnant. Yet there had been no obvious miscarriage or traces of a natural abortion. She had simply ceased to be pregnant.

Kathie was placed under hypnosis by Hopkins' associate Doctor Clamar. During the first session, she recounted how she had wakened in the middle of the night in 1978, and seen two small, grey-faced figures standing by her bed.

At the next session, she went on to describe further how she awoke in bed with her husband, gone to the kitchen, then stood by the sink as if waiting for something. After that, she felt herself floating, with her eyes closed, through the air. Next, she found herself lying down, and seemed to be in the process of being physically examined. She felt two thin probes pressing up her nose, and they seemed to break through the skin in the region of her sinuses. She felt the taste of something like blood. After this, she felt pressure on her abdomen, then on her neck. When she opened her eyes, she saw a small, grey faced man standing next to the table on which she lay. There was a moment of panic, as the man's 'huge black eyes' looked down at her, then she felt suddenly reassured. After this, she seemed to awaken in bed with the two grey figures standing beside them, holding a kind of shimmering box. One of them handed her the box – as in her previous dream – and told her that when she saw it again, she would understand its purpose. After this, she fell asleep.

At this point, Hopkins breaks off his narrative to describe parallel cases. A girl from Kentucky had described to him how, as a five-year-old child, she had been taken by 'little men' into some kind of cold, brightly lit craft, and placed on a table. She was unable to move, and after this, something was inserted up her nose. In another case, a woman from Texas who had been involved in an abduction incident described how some probe had been inserted up her nose with a tiny ball on the end. Hopkins suspected that the ball was somehow left behind after the operation – in other words, that it was some kind of 'implant'.

Hopkins was also intrigued by the fact that the two grey figures appeared to move in absolute unison, and recalled how another abductee who had encountered five tall figures on a lonely road noticed that they all seemed to move simultaneously as they walked towards him. Hopkins comments: 'I do not know what this clonelike appearance and behaviour means, but it is not a constant in abduction reports.'

Further investigation of the incident on 3 October, when Kathie woke up believing that she heard someone call her name, proved that there had been earlier 'incidents'. Before she had gone to bed, she drove to a nearby all-night food store to get something to drink. When she returned, she realised that she had still not bought anything to drink. She turned and drove back – and at this point, saw a large, brightly-lit object in the sky that she assumed was some kind of advertising balloon. It was rolling in a hypnotic manner. After this, she thought she went into the store, but the man she saw there was not like the clerk who usually served her. In fact, she now recognised that the store was not a store, but some kind of spacecraft.

And so, apparently, Kathie had had another 'abduction experience' ten days before she came to New York – and was only able to recollect it under hypnosis. Moreover, she remembered how, after she had fallen asleep in bed, her whole body began to tingle, and she feels herself being examined again.

Back in Copley Woods, she was awakened one night by an awful scream coming from the children's room. Her son Robbie was lying awake, looking shocked. When Kathie told him he must have had a bad dream, he replied 'Mommy, this ain't no dream.' He told her that a man with a big head had come in through the wall and went into her closet, 'and he wouldn't let me move.' The man told him that he wanted his brother Tommy.

She went back to the children's bedroom to look at Tommy, and thought that she saw a flash of light coming from the closet. When she looked, there was nothing there.

A week later, she went into the children's bedroom in the morning, and found Tommy covered with blood. In the hospital, the doctors told her that Tommy had apparently suffered a massive nose bleed in the night – without waking up. An examination of the child's nostrils revealed a small hole high up in his sinus. The doctor thought that Tommy must have pushed a pencil – or some similar object – up his nose.

When Kathie phoned him to tell him about this, Hopkins immediately found himself thinking about the other abductees who had had things inserted up their noses, and suspected that, on the first night when Robbie had seen the man with the big head – the man who said he had 'come for Tommy' – Tommy had been 'anaesthetised' and some kind of implant placed in his nose. Hopkins suspected that this implant had come out a week later, causing the bad nose bleed.

Hopkins also recalled another of his abductee subjects who, at the age of five, was awakened when she heard her name called. She was told to go to the kitchen, where she saw three men in uniforms standing outside the back door. The door opened without anyone touching it, and the men – who had 'bad eyes and no mouth' – picked her up and carried her out. She was taken into a large, metallic object, subjected to some kind of physical examination, and then taken back to her bed. When she woke the next morning, her pyjamas were covered with dried blood – she had had a violent nose bleed in her sleep, so violent that it had clotted the braids of her hair and pooled in her ears.

In 1986, more than two years after Tommy's violent nose bleed, Robbie came into his mother's bedroom and told her there was 'a red tarantula' on the wall of his room. Assuming he had been dreaming, Kathie pulled the bedclothes over him and he went to sleep. But as she lay there in bed watching television, she saw a small, grey skinned figure walk straight past the open door. He appeared to be coming from the children's room.

Another strange event had occurred soon after Tommy's nose bleed. She dreamed that she was lying on a table with her nightgown pulled up under her breasts, while the little man with big eyes examined her. He asked her – telepathically – how she was feeling, and when she said she felt tired and 'kind of crampy' he patted her gently on the stomach and said: 'That's good.' After this, she went back to sleep. But the next morning, she was baffled to find that her panties were lying on top of the bedcovers. She had gone to bed wearing them underneath her nightgown, and certainly had no memory of removing them during the night. That day, she felt pain in her lower abdomen, in the region of her left ovary. It proved to be the day that she was expecting to menstruate. Hopkins suspected that the ovum had been taken from her the previous night.

Now, little by little, these strange events were beginning to come together into a pattern, and Hopkins was disturbed by what he suspected. He happened to know something about the famous abduction experience of Betty and Barney Hill. Although it had not been published in John Fuller's book *The Interrupted Journey*, Barney Hill had described how, during the abduction, a sperm sample was taken from him. And Betty, of course, had described having a long needle inserted into her navel. At that time, no such 'needle' was in use in hospitals. But ten years or so later, there was now a device called a lamaroscope — a long, flexible tube containing fibre optics — that could be inserted into the patient's navel for looking inside her, and also for removing ova for fertilisation as so called 'test tube babies'.

Hopkins was also reminded of the curious experience — described earlier in this book — of Antonio Villas-Boas, the young Brazillian farmer who claimed to have been taken on board a UFO, and being virtually raped by some kind of female alien.

Hopkins writes:

'As the cases have slowly accumulated, the patterns have become clearer. Over the past six years I have worked with four male abductees who have described encounters very similar to Villas-Boas's abduction, and three others whose incomplete account strongly suggests such an event. The female side of this equation, which we will examine later on, is more complex. It should be pointed out, however, that I know of *no* case in which a female abductee has ever reported an act of intercourse. Above all, in none of these cases involving either men or women do we have what can be called a basically *erotic* experience. The descriptions are invariably of a detached, clinical procedure instead, even if some of them result in more or less involuntary ejaculation.

'Now all of this leads to the unwelcome speculative inference that somewhere, somehow, human beings — or possibly hybrids of some sort — are being produced by a technology obviously — yet not inconceivably — superior to ours. And if that possibility is not enough to induce paranoia in the heartiest, consider this: With our own current technology of genetic engineering expanding day by day, is it not conceivable that an advanced alien technology may already have the ability to remove ovum and sperm from human beings, experimentally alter their genetic structure, and then *replant* altered and fertilised ova back into unknowing host females to be carried to term? Ova that can be removed can also be replaced, even by our own present-day medical technology.'

In short, Hopkins suspects that what is happening is that female abductees are being artificially inseminated, possibly by male sperm taken from other abductees, allowed to carry the foetus for some time, and then subjected to another operation which removes the foetus.

When Hopkins visited Kathie in Copley Woods, she said something that confirmed this suspicion. When he remarked how lucky she was to have two boys like Tommy and Robbie, she stopped the car and said: 'Budd, you know I have a daughter too.' She went on: 'I know I have a daughter. I think I've even seen her. I know what she looks like.'

It was when Kathie visited New York for a second time that Hopkins realised that one of the earlier incidents she had described was more significant than it seemed. Kathie had earlier described how, as a teenager, she was driving around late at night with two girlfriends when they saw a UFO. At this point, Kathie's memory seemed to blur, and all she could remember was feeling 'frozen' in the car, unable to move. Her friend Dorothy seemed to have a memory of getting out of the car, and then could both remember their friend Roberta crouching in the back seat and refusing to look. After this, Kathie had arrived home far later than she expected.

Under hypnosis, Kathie remembered this event in more detail. It was at the time that she had just met her future husband.

Now, under hypnosis, Kathie was able to remember how they sat looking up at the light in the sky, until it seemed to be right over them, looking like 'an airplane with the strobe things on it'. After this there was a flash in the car, and Kathie describes how she suddenly became very cold. Everything became black, and she wanted to get out of the car, but was unable to move. She explained that her back felt stiff and that her arms and legs felt cold and heavy. She seemed to be held down by an invisible force. Finally, she recollects getting out of the car, and standing beside Dorothy, watching something float off into the sky.

At this point in the hypnosis, Hopkins took her back to the flash in the car. He suspected that Kathie had been abducted first, and then returned to the car, after which her friend Dorothy was abducted. In fact, Kathie now began to remember some kind of pain that 'makes my stomach hurt. It feels like my legs are being pulled off my body from the waist down.'

As Kathie moans in pain, Hopkins asks her where the pain is situated. 'Where my uterus is, down low, like I'm going to have my period. It's hard, it hurts. It's like a toothache . . . Oh it feels like someone's pushing on me *real hard* . . . Wiggling and pushing right in there.' She explains that it feels like 'a finger' right above her bladder.

This, Hopkins came to believe, was the point at which she was artificially impregnated. And the baby was taken away in the following March, when she woke up and found herself menstruating.

Later, still under hypnosis, Kathie described how she was again lying on a couch, apparently undergoing some kind of pelvic examination. Suddenly, she tell Hopkins: 'I just want to scream.' When he asks if she means scream from the pain, she suddenly says in a high wailing voice: 'No! It's not right, it's not fair! IT'S NOT FAIR! IT'S MINE! IT'S MINE! I HATE YOU. I HATE YOU! . . . IT'S NOT FAIR!'

This, Hopkins realised, was the moment when her baby was taken away.

Later still, Kathie explained what she meant when she had said that she had a daughter and that she had seen her.

She had awakened in a place that was 'all white', and that there were several of these 'little grey guys' around her. She was standing up, and one of them had his arm around her waist, as if to comfort her. At this point, a little girl came into the room, escorted by two of the grey men. 'She looked to be about four. She looked about Tommy's size . . . She was real pretty. She looked like an elf, or an . . . angel. She had really big blue eyes and a little teeny-weeny nose, just so perfect. And her mouth was just so perfect and tiny, and she was pale, except her lips were pink and her eyes were blue. And her hair was white and wispy and thin . . . fine . . . real thin and fine. Her head was a little larger than normal, 'specially not in the forehead and back here . . . The forehead was a little bit bigger . . . but she was just a doll. And they brought her to me. And they stood there, and they looked at me. Everyone was looking at me. And I looked at her, and I wanted to hold her. She was just so pretty, and I felt like I just wanted to hold her. And I started crying . . .'

Before the grey men took the child away, they told Kathie that she would see her again.

Under hypnosis, she was able to recollect how the little grey man whom she thought of as the child's 'father' held her hand, 'and I feel all kinds of things . . . sad, and warm, and care, and distance . . . and goodbye . . . and lonely . . . I feel lonely too.'

When she was awake, she expanded on this final experience. 'You know, when he looked at me and held my hand I got this rush of emotion that I didn't know where it came from. It was lonely and sad and sorry, but love and caring and happiness and satisfaction – and guilt – all at once. I didn't think it was coming from me. Why would I feel guilt?' Hopkins said that perhaps it was his guilt she was aware of. 'Yes, it wasn't my guilt. He felt sad and lonely, but he felt satisfied and happy, and he cared, about me, as a living thing. He was going to miss me as much as I was going to miss her.' She adds, he wanted me to be happy at the success like he was, and he felt guilty that I felt that way . . .'

This, then, is Hopkins thesis. The 'aliens' – little grey men with large heads and big black eyes – are somehow using human beings to create hybrids. In a chapter called 'Other Women, Other Men', he goes on to describe a number of other cases that seem to echo the one he has already described. A subject called Andrea had told him how she was 'floated out of her bed', into a UFO. There, as she sat paralysed on the table, a long needle was pressed up her nose, causing her pain as it broke through the top of her nasal cavity. When she woke up in the morning, there was blood on her nightgown and the bedclothes from a bad nose bleed.

Andrea accounted for a scar on her chest by explaining that when she was about six years old, she could recall lying on a table in a small, round room lit by pink light, and a small man doing something to her chest. Hopkins' female assistant Louise later saw a thin red cut three and a half inches long down the centre of Andrea's back.

But Andrea had had an even stranger experience. When she was thirteen, and still a virgin, she became pregnant. At this time she did not even have a boyfriend. She dreamed that she was having sex with a man who had no hair on his head and 'real funny eyes'. 'I've just felt something in me, something sharp, and then my vagina felt like it was on fire . . . In the morning my underpants were all wet and the bed was wet, and I felt all burning.

'And after a while my stomach started to grow. My mother took me to a gynecologist, and I was pregnant. I couldn't believe it. My father was furious and asked who did it to me, he wanted to get even. I told him it was a weird man in a dream, with funny eyes and a big head. And you know, Budd, the gynecologist said I was still a virgin. I still had my hymen.' The situation was resolved when Andrea had an abortion.

Another one of Hopkins' subjects, a girl called Susan, described a similar experience when she was in Austria as a young woman in 1953. She was sixteen at the time, and had stopped her car to watch a strange, darting light in the sky. She then began to feel some kind of telepathic communication between herself and the UFO. She felt herself rising vertically off the road, floating upwards until she came to rest on her back on a table inside the UFO. She was relaxed and unafraid, although she was naked from the waist down. She felt two small clips being attached to her labia, spreading them apart, and then a thin probe moving up inside her. It seems that the purpose of this operation was not to impregnate her, but to examine her internally.

She told Hopkins that a year after this experience, she told her boyfriend about her experience. At this point, Susan decided to ring the boyfriend to see whether he could remember the conversation. In fact, he could not recall it, but *did* remind her of a UFO sighting they had made together at that time. She had totally forgotten about this sighting.

As a result of further questioning, Hopkins came to the conclusion that both Susan and her boyfriend had shared an abduction experience at some point. He suspected that, at the age of sixteen, she was impregnated, and that later, that baby was removed.

Another abductee called Pam described under hypnosis how she and her sister had seen a 'low, silver-grey vehicle' pull up beside their car when they had broken down, and that her mind had then become confused. Later, when she was married and living in New Mexico, she had a recurrent nightmare involving a 'silver train' which was coming down from the sky to take her away. And although she was practising birth control at this time, she suddenly found herself pregnant. Medical tests confirmed this, and she decided to have an abortion. But when she went to the clinic — apparently two months pregnant — the doctor told her that there was no sign whatever that she had ever been pregnant.

Hopkins goes on to describe some curious experiences of male abductees he has interviewed. A man he calls Ed wrote him a letter telling him that he was a roving mechanic at a mine, and that one night, dozing in his truck, he had suddenly found himself 'frozen' and unable to move. When he read Hopkins' *Missing Time*, he began to suspect that he had had some kind of UFO experience during this period of paralysis. Under hypnosis, he was able to remember it.

He was just about to go to sleep in the truck when a bright light dazzled him. After this, he felt weightless, and floated up through the air. He was taken into a UFO — let in through the door. Its inhabitants, who had round heads and thin features, made him lie down on a table, naked, and then examined him carefully all over. He noticed that they seemed to have a particular interest in his genital region.

The following day, when his wife was not present, Ed told the rest of the story. A woman was brought into the room, 'built more like a human being . . . she had mamm-aries, but she didn't have any body hair at all. Her head was larger than a normal woman's would be.'

Ed explained that he was lying on his back, naked, 'and somehow they made me erect and she mounted me . . . she rode me and she was on top of me until I orgasmed, and then she got off and left the room and the two guys, they took little spoons and scraped the left over semen off my penis and took it as a sample in a bottle and kept it.'

Hopkins wanted to know how they had caused him to have an erection, and Ed replied: 'God, this is preposterous, but it seems they stuck like a vacuum devise on my penis.'

When he came out of his trance, he noticed that his abducters seemed angry – the reason being that he had had a vasectomy two years before, and therefore was sterile.

As a result of telling Hopkins about this experience, Ed recalled an earlier abduction. He had felt a sudden urge to go into the back yard in the middle of the night, and the small men emerged from the woods, and somehow paralysed him. In the UFO, a suction devise was put on his penis, and the result was that he reached ejaculation – apparently without any kind of sexual excitement. This may have been the reason that the abductors returned a few years later and took him off for a second sample – only to find that he was now sterile. After this experience, Ed explained that he was left with a deep, aching sensation in the region of his pubic bone.

Ed then recalled two earlier abduction experiences, one when he was a child of five, and one when he was a teenager. This leads Hopkins to comment:

'One of the major findings described in my book *Missing Time* was an apparent programme of systematically repeated abductions of the same individuals over many years. The analogy mentioned earlier that comes to mind is our programme of zoological study in which wild animals are captured and tranquilised to allow the permanent attachment of small transmitters or even simple tags before they are released back into their natural environments. The transmitters allow scientists to track their movements and thus to learn the species' migration patterns, grazing habits and other useful information. This analogy is obviously anthropomorphic, but it is nevertheless suggested, especially since there is evidence that tiny implants are put in place in UFO abduction cases, as we have seen.'

Hopkins goes on to cite the experience of another abductee, a man he calls Dan, a factory worker from Ohio. Dan wrote to Hopkins in some distress, saying that he had had some kind of disturbing experience. When Hopkins finally went to see him, he discovered that Dan's abduction experiences had dated from early childhood.

He had been with a group of people when several of them were taken into a UFO. He describes lying on a table, with his legs spread wide apart, while his abductors 'put something on my genital area. It looks kinda clear, a conical shape, it covers up the whole area. There's a sensation, of vibrating. It didn't hurt. I just feel that vibrating, and it seems like a shock. I don't know. Kind of like a pleasant shock. . . . I could feel it touching the end of my penis, and right around the whole area. It felt kinda cold.' As he ejaculated, he experienced an odd electrical sensation in his head.

Hopkins suggests that this electrical sensation could be some kind of 'artificial neurological trigger for the sexual release.' He mentions another abductee who had also had some kind of clear plastic covering placed over his genitals, felt a vibration, then the sudden rush of the orgasm, and the sense that his semen had been taken as a sample.

Hopkins also explores the question of the 'paralysis' that the abductors seem to be able to induce at will. Kathie Davis had also experienced something of the sort in her teens. She described to Hopkins how she made a trip to Kentucky when she was sixteen with the family of her girlfriend Nan. They had stayed in a cabin at the side of a lake. Nan's father had a Citizen-Band radio in his car, and the girls somehow got into contact with a group of boys who were also using a CB radio. While Kathie was still sitting in front of the radio, the boys — three of them — suddenly arrived in a car. The odd thing was that, although the track was bumpy and pitted, the car seemed to glide as smoothly as if it was on a tarmac road. Kathie was puzzled about how the boys had succeeded in finding them — they had given them no instructions.

When she took the three boys indoors — one of them was blonde, and did most of the talking — they discovered that everybody was still awake, in spite of the lateness of the hour. They seemed to be standing there, as if they were waiting for something.

The 'boys' sat down and drank beer, and the conversation went on for hours. Kathie apparently found the blonde boy extremely attractive.

The next day, Kathie and Nan went to the place where the boys claimed they were camping, but found no camping site in the area.

Hopkins was greatly struck by Kathie's description of taking the boys into the cabin. 'I was sure some of them would have been in bed, since it was late, but they were all up, just sitting there or standing, and the TV wasn't even on. But Budd, they were just *still*, you know, not moving, like they were hardly awake, and not saying anything. And my head started to feel funny, between my eyes, and then the blonde guy spoke and everyone kind of came to life, and began to move and talk. It was really weird, like they had been asleep or something.'

Hopkins summarises some of his conclusions in the final chapter of the book.

'And behind the abduction phenomenon as it has been described by literally hundreds of witnesses there seems to be a very peculiar and very consistant ethical position. In none of the cases I've investigated have I ever encountered

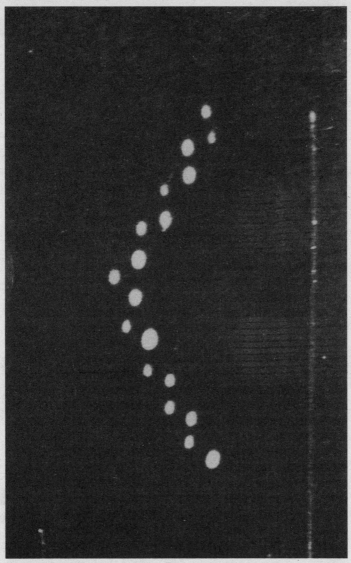

Pictures of the 'Lubbock Lights' taken by Carl Hart in Lubbock, Texas on August 30th, 1951

even the suggestion of deliberate harm or malevolence. The abductees are apparently kept as calm as possible and seem to suffer only minimal physical pain – a situation not unlike that of a well-run dental office. People are picked up, examined, samples are taken and so on, and then they are returned more or less intact to the place where the abduction began. There seems to be a definite effort by the UFO occupants to make the operations as swift, efficient, and painless as possible. There is reason to believe that the partial amnesia which often accompanies these experiences is intended to help the abductees continue their normal lives as much as it is to conceal UFO activities.'

And yet, Hopkins points out, most abductees *do* suffer some kind of harm. One woman who had suffered several abduction experiences as a child attempted to kill herself when she was ten. It was only later that she realised that she was suffering a deep sense of dread because of her abduction experiences – which she had consciously forgotten.

Hopkins seems to feel that the abductors are curiously naive. 'In one case I've investigated, a Minnesota man and his wife were abducted together; the husband was forced to watch helplessly while a long needle was run into the navel of his paralysed wife. His abductors were completely surprised by his fury and hatred. "But we *want* you to see what we're doing," they explained ingenuously. "We are not harming your mate. Why are you angry?" '

It would seem, Hopkins points out, that the aliens are oddly emotionless beings who cannot comprehend why their scientific experiments should upset their human victims. 'Their psychology, if one can use the term, does not make any more sense to us than human psychology apparently makes to them.'

So, according to Hopkins, the abductors are neither evil aliens, bent on destroying the human race, nor benevolent 'visitors from space', whose only purpose is to aid the evolution of the human race. Whatever they're doing seems rather more complicated.

Another disturbing aspect is the sheer *number* of such cases. Hopkins describes how, after he appeared on a tv programme with two abductees, the station was suddenly flooded with phone calls and letters from people who all suspected that they had been abductees.

> Ruth May Weber, of Yucca Valley, California, had a psychic experience involving aliens. She heard a voice telling her that Earth was already inhabited by thousands of space people, who would take over in the event of some great world catastrophe. Later, walking through the street of her home town, she suddenly saw showers of space people floating down through the air, and then disappearing into the crowd, entirely unnoticed by the citizens of Yucca Valley.

Next to Budd Hopkins, the best known investigator of UFO abductions is probably Doctor David M. Jacobs, who is a historian specialising in 20th century America. Jacobs became interested in UFOs in the early sixties, when he was a student at the University of Wisconsin. When, in 1966, he read John Fuller's *The Interrupted Journey*, about Barney and Betty Hill, he was sceptical – it seemed to him far more likely that the 'memories' of abduction had been induced by the hypnosis.

As a historian, he was inclined to concentrate on trying to find historical patterns in the phenomena. He at first found the sheer diversity of the reports bewildering – two men who claimed to have been abducted by creatures with skin like elephants and long sharp noses and hands like claws; one who claimed to have been abducted not only by aliens but by a human being as well; a woman who said she had been transported to another planet, and various abductees who reported Benevolent Beings who had come to teach the human race how to live at peace.

The turning point came when he met Budd Hopkins in 1982, and decided that he would have to begin doing hypnotic regression himself.

In 1986, he tried his skills on his first abductee – a woman he calls Melissa Bucknell. She had been hypnotised before, so his nervousness was unnecessary – she quickly went into a trance. Then she described how, as a six-year-old child playing in a field near her home, she was transported into a UFO by aliens. Her clothes were removed and a physical examination was performed, including probing her vagina with a needle-like instrument. She felt that something had been implanted near her left ovary.

Soon, Jacobs had a large number of regular 'patients', and during the next five years, conducted more than 325 hypnotic sessions.

His approach to the question was basically statistical. Rather than describing particular abductions in some detail, like Budd Hopkins, he prefers to list the phenomena under various headings, like 'Getting There, Physical Probing, Alien Bonding, and The Breeding Programme.'

In his book *Secret Life* (1992), published in paperback as *Alien Encounters*, he gives a basic picture of what happens to so many people.

'An unsuspecting woman is in her room preparing to go to bed. She gets into bed, reads a while, turns off the light, and drifts into a peaceful night's sleep. In the middle of the night she turns over and lies on her back. She is awakened by a light that seems to be glowing in her room. The light moves towards her bed and takes the shape of a small "man" with a bald head and huge black eyes. She is terrified. She wants to run but she cannot move. She wants to scream but she cannot speak. The "man" moves towards her and looks deeply into her eyes. Suddenly she is calmer, and she "knows" that the "man" is not going to hurt her.'

After this, the abductee finds himself or herself floating up through the air, and then into the spacecraft, where he or she is examined on some kind of table, by small creatures with large heads and huge black eyes that slant a little like a cat's. There are also usually some Taller Beings, inches to a foot higher, and who seem to have authority over the smaller beings — like a doctor over nurses; they may intervene if the abductee shows himself to be angry or difficult, or needs to be physically restrained.

The room may contain other tables, with other human beings lying on them, usually in a kind of semi-anaesthetised state. One abductee described a hall with about two hundred 'beds' in it. A lengthy examination usually follows — not unlike the kind of examination conducted by a doctor for an insurance company — except that it seems to be far more searching.

Jacobs also notes that the aliens seem to indulge in a kind of activity that he calls 'Mindscan'. This is usually carried out by one of the 'Taller Beings'. They seem to play a more authoritative role in the process of examination. 'Mindscan' involves staring deep into the eye of the abductee, so that the latter feel as if some kind of information has been extracted from their minds.

During this process, what Jacobs calls 'Bonding' often occurs. This is the feeling that was described by Kathie Davis when she talked to the being she felt to be the 'father' of her child — a sense of close kinship. The result is not unlike the 'transference' phenomenon in psychotherapy —

when the patient falls in love with the doctor and places him on a pedestal. When it happens to small children, they become convinced that the Taller Being is a friend who can be totally trusted. One abductee, under hypnosis, described how when she was twelve, she looked into the eyes of one of the Taller Beings, and experienced a sensation of love in which there was a definite sexual component. 'He looked into my eyes, and I really liked him. . . . I just felt happy and I just lay down.'

After this, females may experience some kind of implant. One said indignantly: 'I feel like a cow. I'm so mad . . .' When this abductee awoke the next morning in her bed, she found a sticky gelatinous substance between her legs, which she washed off in the shower.

Males often experience the kind of 'sperm extraction' described by Budd Hopkins. A cup-like machine is placed over the penis, also covering the scrotum. After this, sexual arousal is experienced, while the alien may press or 'knead' the right side of the lower abdomen. 'That's when I ejaculate . . . I think while one little guy hooks up the machine the other one pumps my stomach for some reason. . . . when he looks into my eyes, I get this bonding feeling. When the machine's all hooked up and ready, he strokes me or something. It feels pleasurable. And I ejaculate into the machine.' Another comments: 'There's an erection and there's no sense of release or anything orgasmic; it is just like a literal drawing out.' In other words, the sperm-extractor seems to have something in common with a milking machine used on cows.

The aliens also seem to be able to cause imagery to arise in the mind of the abductee, often associated with some powerful emotion – one woman relived the experience of being beside her mother when she was dying of cancer. Another abductee who was subjected to a powerful 'envisioning' process said:

'They gave me some pretty vivid images . . . but they didn't do it in that room, they put me in a little room with a chair. Just one chair in the middle . . . and I sat on the chair and they put this scope on my head. It looked something like what they looked at me in. It's real bright now. It seems like a bright room and they told me terrible things would happen to the Earth and that it would just blow up, and cities would crumble and mountains would fall and the sun would be black. And they said that it's bad because people can't stop being greedy and that they were doing something to help us, and I don't know how . . . they were horrible images, the images I still see in nightmares. I have recurring nuclear war dreams.'

He is asked: 'What are they doing while you are receiving these images?'

The abductee explains that one of them is holding an instrument like a telescope or kaleidoscope up against his forehead. This, he thought, was to enable the alien to look at images in his mind. And he feels that when the being looks into his eyes, 'I think he's looking into my soul.'

The aliens appear to be able to induce illusions. One female abductee was told to sit down on a couch, in front of a table with a flower-pot on it. A number of human guards were standing around. A male to whom she was very attracted was brought into the room and she was astonished to see him. He came over and leaned forward to kiss her, so that she had the feeling that they were going to make love. But looking around, she suddenly realised that the human guards were actually aliens, and that the male who was about to kiss her was also an alien. The purpose of these 'staged' scenes appears to be psychological study of the individual concerned.

Like Kathy Davis, many abductees are brought into contact with alien babies, or foetuses often, the abductee is required to hold a baby and establish some kind of physical contact. One abductee suggested that she thought the purpose of this exercise was to give the alien baby some experience of 'touching'. Both Hopkins and Jacobs point out that it has been discovered that touching is essential to all babies — animal and well as human. Without touching, normal development can be unsatisfactory and greatly retarded. Jacobs observes the abductee often feels that some of the babies are hers, and that she is a part of some grand scheme, and has reason to feel proud of herself. One male abductee was introduced to a little girl who reminded him of his neice. As she reached up and touched his cheek — 'like a little poke' — he experienced a sense of 'joining'. When the child was taken away, he became deeply upset, although the aliens appeared to find this baffling. Finally, one of the taller beings stared at him, and somehow made him calm down.

In one strange procedure, abductees are made to climb into a kind of pool, and they find that they can actually breathe under the liquid, which seems to be more gelatinous than water.

Hopkins' observation that normal sexual activity never seems to occur in abduction situations is contradicted by Jacobs. One young woman described how she was taken to a male abductee, who was lying, apparently unconscious, on the table. The aliens wanted her to get on top of him. In spite of her unwillingness, she is made to climb on to his erection, and move up and down on him until he ejaculates inside her. When she moves off him, he remains erect.

One fifteen-year-old girl had some kind of head gear attached to her, which induced powerful sexual feelings. Since she was inexperienced, she did not understand these. After this, a middle-aged man with a paunch is brought in, his eyes glazed over and unfocussed. One of the Taller Beings makes her body respond sexually after this, 'this guy climbs on top of me, and he's moving and it . . . doesn't make any sense, but it feels like he starts to climax and doesn't finish, or he gets to the point of coming, but what's the point of that? . . . they just pull him off, and stick something up where he was, a metal thing it feels like.'

Another thirteen-year-old girl was told that she was now 'ripe' and that she should go and breed. After that, they brought in a teenage boy who also seemed to be in a trance, and who climbed on her and ruptured her hymen. This happened to her on two occasions while she was still a teenager.

There are also occasions when the alien has sex with the abductee. In that case, the abductee is somehow made to believe that the person who is making love to her is her husband or someone she loves. The alien's face may change into that of the husband. 'The insertion of the "penis" is quick, and the penis does not feel normal; it is usually very thin and very short. The normal thrusting movement does not take place, but the woman feels a sudden "pulse". Then it is all over. "We have no clear evidence that the aliens have genitals, but hybrids sometimes do".'

In the remainder of his book, Jacobs examines in some detail other aspects of the abduction experience – how the abductee finds himself or herself back home, the appearance and behaviour of the aliens, the psychological problems that may result from the abduction, even if the abductee experiences total amnesia about it.

Like Hopkins, Jacobs observes how often female abductees experience unplanned pregnancies. The woman is often deeply puzzled and disturbed because she is not engaged in sex, or has taken full birth control precautions. Then, a few months later, the pregnancy suddenly vanishes, with no kind of discharge or miscarriage.

David Jacobs' work is remarkable for its analytical breakdown of the abduction phenomenon, and for the extreme care with which he documents various aspects. Yet at the end of the book, in a kind of question-and-answer session, he answers the question: 'Why do aliens repeatedly abduct the same people?'. 'We do not know the answer to this.'

The latest 'respectable' addition to the ranks of the UFO researchers is Doctor John E. Mack, Professor of Psychiatry at Harvard medical school, and the author of a classic biography of Lawrence of Arabia. At the beginning of his book *Abduction* (1994), he describes how a colleague asked him if he wanted to meet Budd Hopkins, and he replied 'Who's he?' When told that Hopkins was a New York artist who interviewed people who claimed to have been abducted by aliens in space ships, Mack replied that he must be crazy. Finally, in January 1990, he was introduced to Hopkins by his colleague.

After Mack had interviewed four abductees, and heard the same stories of their encounters with aliens, he began to conclude that perhaps, after all, they were telling the truth.

After this, Hopkins began to refer to him cases that took place in the Boston area, and during the course of the next three and a half years, he saw over a hundred persons, of whom seventy-six (whose ages ranged from fifty-seven to two) fulfilled his 'quite strict criteria for an abduction case: conscious recall or recall with the help of hypnosis, of being taken by alien beings into a strange craft, reported with emotion appropriate to the experience being described and no apparently mental condition that could account for the story.'

Typical of the cases cited by Mack is that of a twenty-two-year-old music student whom he calls Catherine. In February 1991, she had started to drive home from a nightclub where she worked as receptionist, but experienced an odd desire to go for a drive. When she returned home, she realised that there seemed to be a forty-five minute period for which she could not account. The next day, when she woke up, the television news mentioned that someone had seen a UFO over Boston, and a map of the object's path showed that it seemed to be travelling in the direction in which she had driven. A violent nosebleed — the first of her life — led her to feel that something strange had happened.

Under hypnosis, Catherine recalled that her first abduction experience had happened when she was three years old. She was awakened in the middle of the night and saw some 'being' at her bedroom window with a blue light streaming in behind it. It had 'huge black eyes, a pointed chin — his entire head is like a teardrop inverted. He's got a line for a mouth, nose I can't see . . . It's just a bump. He doesn't seem to be wearing any clothes.' The being came into the room, and Catherine was 'floated' through the window and taken to a disc-shaped ship outside. In a large room, with several older children, she was asked by a woman who reminded her of a nursery school teacher whether she wanted to play. The teacher then produced a kind of metallic ball which floated around the room and handed her a metallic rod with a short antenna coming out of the top. This rod was apparently able to control the metal ball, to make it stop or move around or hover, but this also required considerable concentration. Catherine did so well at it that she sensed the other children were jealous and angry. Catherine was unable to recall more of this episode, although she could remember that something else had happened.

The next encounter occurred when she was seven. She was walking down an alleyway when she saw 'a little white thing', which turned out to be a man with a big bald head and big eyes. He told her he wanted to take her somewhere, and she objected because her parents had told her not to go with strange people. Nevertheless, he took her arm and they flew up through the air and in through a hole — presumably in a UFO — and into a room. There, he told her that he was going to make a little cut in her finger because he needed a sample. She protested vociferously, in spite of which he made a little cut on the forefinger of her left hand, and took a blood sample. He explained that he was researching 'your planet'. 'We're trying to stop the damage from pollution.' Then Catherine found herself once again back in the alleyway, and when she rejoined some friends watching cartoons on television, no one had noticed that she had been absent for a quarter of an hour.

Finally, under hypnosis, she was able to recall what had happened when she lost the forty-five minutes in February 1991. She had driven into a wooded area, and stopped, after which she experienced a kind of paralysis. Something opened the driver's door, and guided her out of the car.

She was taken up into a huge ship, where several aliens tried to remove her clothes. She got angry, and asked them why they didn't go and rent a porn movie. Then it dawned on her that they didn't know what a porn movie was, and did not understand the concept of voyeurism.

After this, she was taken into an enormous room 'the size of an airplane hanger', in which there were hundreds of tables, and hundreds of human beings lying on them. After the usual physical examination, during which a black-eyed alien soothed her and made her feel better, a metal tube was inserted in her vagina, and then another thinner instrument was used to reach up inside her. When it came out again, it seemed to be holding something like a foetus. Her guess was that it must be about three months old.

The aliens seemed unable to understand her anger at being treated in this way, and she was finally 'floated' back to her car.

It had been her impression that the foetus was about three months old. When John Mack asked her about this, she recalled how, about three months before the episode, she had found herself driving in the middle of the night along deserted roads, and had pulled off the highway at a rest stop. She thinks she sat there for about fifteen minutes – with a sensation as if she was waiting for something – and when nothing happened, drove off home again. It now struck her as possible that this was the time when she was 'impregnated'.

As a result of her hypnotic sessions with John Mack, Catherine found that she was able to come to terms – to some extent – with what was happening to her. The sense of outrage began to give way to a feeling of curiosity about what the aliens wanted to achieve. She also noted that her intuitions had improved, and that she can feel 'auras', and is more attuned to the emotional states of other people. 'This whole experience makes you open up to so many levels, so many other possibilities. Everyone has these kinds of abilities, but we shut them off . . .'

In July 1991, Catherine told John Mack that she believed something had happened two nights before. At a hypnotic session, she was finally able to describe this. A light, like a huge searchlight, streamed into her bedroom, and she passed through the window, the porch and a tree and saw her apartment building receding below her. She entered through a hole in the floor of the craft, and was taken into a kind of conference room, which she knew to be an illusion implanted in her mind. This was verified when the conference room melted away to reveal the actual room they were in. When she objected that they had concocted the conference room for her benefit, she was told: 'We have to have a conference, so you have to think its a conference, so we're taking you to a conference room so that you can be in that kind of serious frame of mind instead of making your usual smart-ass remarks that you always do.' Catherine commented: 'When this happened, I was just starting not to fight them. I was just at the very beginning. I'm not where I am now . . .'

After this, she was shown scenes of nature on a screen including the Grand Canyon. After this, there were pyramids, pictures of pharoahs and hieroglyphics. After this, they showed her a picture of a tomb painting, then she saw herself painting it. In this earlier incarnation she was a man, and she felt: 'this makes sense to me . . . this is not a trick.'

Mack questioned her at some length about her life as a painter, and was struck by the amount she seemed to know — for example about the process of mixing paint, about the man's clothing and head-dress. During this process, Catherine apparently became the painter, whom she called Akremenon. She was able to describe in detail precisely what she was painting, the different sized figures on the panel (royalty had to be larger than commoners) and the problems of proportion involved. She said that the pharoah for whom she was working had 'demoted' various gods, and Mack speculates that it could have been the pharaoh Akhenaton.

Now, for the first time, Catherine began to feel that the aliens were offering her something that she could understand. When she asked them why they used such 'theatrics' they explained: 'To make you understand, to comprehend the implications. To put you in the right frame of mind.' She came to feel that certain emotions like love, caring, helpfulness, compassion are 'the key', whereas others like anger, hatred and fear are 'not useful', especially fear. 'Fear is like the worst one. They were trying to get me to get over fear, and that's why they were trying to scare me so badly, because I would eventually get sick of it, and get over it, and get on to the more important things.'

As a result of her new attitude, Catherine was able to play a more active part in the abductee support group conducted by Mack.

There is a sense in which Mack's attitude to the whole abduction phenomenon is more creative and positive than that of any other investigator. 'A number of abductees with whom I have worked experience at certain points an opening up to the sort of being in the cosmos, which they often call Home, and from which they feel they have been brutally cut off in the course of becoming embodied as a human being. They may weep ecstatically when during our sessions they experience an opening or return to Home. They may . . . rather resent having to remain on Earth in embodied form, even as they realise that on Earth they have some sort of mission to assist in bringing about a change in human consciousness.'

In speaking of the philosophical implications of the abduction experience, Mack writes: 'Quite a few abductees have spoken to me of their sense that at least some of their experiences are not occurring within the physical space/time dimensions of the universe as we comprehend it. They speak of aliens breaking through from another dimension, through a "slit" or "crack" in some sort of barrier, entering our world from "beyond the veil". Abductees, some of whom have little education to prepare them to explain about such abstractions or odd dislocations, will speak of the collapse of space/time that occurs during their experiences. They experience the aliens, indeed their abductions themselves, as happening in another reality, although one that is as powerfully actual to them as — or more so than — the familiar physical world.' One of his abductees said: 'You can't really evaluate it in the language and physical descriptive terms of this dimension because it wasn't really happening here. It was half happening here and half happening somewhere else.' Catherine had told him that she remembered some place between times of incarnation on Earth where bodies were not solid, appearing only in kind of energy outline. 'This was before any of us had lives here. This place is in a totally different universe. It's not in our earth space/time dimension.' Another abductee said: 'All times can come to one place. This is real. It's not philosophical. I can really go to another time frame and [my experiences] can pull me from other time frames to here.'

In a section entitled 'Spiritual Implications' Mack compares the abductors to Zen Buddist masters who use shock treatment as a teaching method. 'The alien beings that abductees speak about seem to many of them to come from another domain that is felt to be closer to the source of being or primary creation. They have been described, however homely their appearance, as intermediaries or emissaries from God, even as angels . . . the acknowledgement of their existence, after the initial ontological shock, is sometimes . . . the first step in the opening of consciousness to a universe that is no longer simply material. Abductees come to appreciate that the universe is filled with intelligences and is itself intelligent. They develop a sense of awe before a mysterious cosmos that becomes sacred and ensouled. The sense of separation from all the rest of creation breaks down and the experience of oneness becomes an essential aspect of the evolution of the abductees' consciousness . . .' He adds: 'The aliens themselves may come to be seen as a split-off part of the abductees' soul or Self.'

In a section called 'FURTHER IMPLICATIONS FOR HUMAN CONSCIOUSNESS', Mack writes: 'Abduction experiences also open the consciousness of abductees, as I work with them, to cycles of birth and death that are reminiscent of the Tibetan transitional realities or *Bardos*. This is most clearly illustrated in the past life experiences that are emerging increasingly in our sessions as I have become willing to listen to them. These reports suggest that individual consciousness may have its own line of development, separate from the body.'

It is significant that Mack associates some of these implications with the ideas put forward by his friend Thomas Kuhn, the author of the influential *Structure of*

Scientific Revolutions. Kuhn argues that scientists imagine that science is a 'wide open' discipline, whose only purpose is to expand human knowledge, and whose approach is always free of prejudice. Kuhn suggests that, on the contrary, scientists are inclined to develop an unconscious attitude which is closer to that of orthodox churchmen, outraged by anyone who does not accept their basic dogmas. He goes on to suggest that what he calls 'paradigm shifts' only come about as a result of violent upheavals, which sometimes involve individual scientists being treated as pariahs and outcasts.

Mack argues that 'the experiences recounted by the abductees with whom I have worked during the past four years constitute, I think, a rich body of evidence to support the idea that the cosmos, far from being devoid of meaning and intelligence, is . . . "informed by some kind of universal intelligence", an intelligence "of scarely conceivable power, complexity and aesthetic subtlety yet one to which the human intelligence is akin, and in which it can participate".'

John Mack's view is supported by the widely publicised books of another abductee, Whitley Strieber. In *Communion, a True Story,* (1987) Strieber describes his own experiences of abduction, beginning — apparently — on 26 December, 1985, in his secluded log cabin in up-state New York. He woke up in the middle of the night with a sense that something was wrong, and saw an 'alien visitor' coming in through the door. It was about three foot six inches tall, had the usual oval shaped head, and enormous black eyes set at a slant. After this, he was taken out of the house, and into some kind of spacecraft. His impression was that the alien who seemed to be in charge was female. He was shown a box containing a kind of thin hypodermic needle, and told that this was going to be inserted into his brain. His reaction was to scream, and when the woman asked him: 'What can we do to make you stop screaming?',

His reply was: 'You could let me smell you.' (He admits that many of his reactions and responses seem, in restrospect, to be completely illogical, like those in a dream.)

He was undressed, and laid down on a table with his legs apart, after which some kind of device was inserted into his rectum. After this, they made an incision in his forefinger. Suddenly he found himself back in his bed, with no memory whatsoever of what had happened. It seemed to him that a barn owl had looked in through his window, but when he looked at the roof, he saw there were no tracks in the snow.

For some time before this, Strieber and his wife had been experiencing a great deal of conflict, due to – as he acknowledges – 'my demands and accusatory behaviour'. 'At the time I had no idea that I was suffering from emotional trauma, or that dozens of other people had been through very similar ordeals after being taken by the visitors.'

He found that his ability to concentrate suddenly vanished. He experienced a sudden pain behind his right ear, and his wife noticed a tiny pinpoint of a scab.

Reading a book called *Science and the UFOs* he suddenly found that he was unable to go on reading, and had to slam it shut.

His suspician that he had been abducted finally led him to contact Budd Hopkins, who, it turned out, lived only a few blocks away from him in New York.

From this point on, Strieber's account echoes that of many other abductees. Hypnosis by Doctor Donald Klein, who had had no experience of abductees, and therefore could not ask leading questions, gradually began to uncover a whole series of abduction experiences that had been taking place since his childhood. There were whole days – in one case weeks – of 'missing time'. He became increasingly certain that his wife and son had also been abducted or had some contact with the aliens.

Participation in a 'abduction support group' made him aware that there were dozens – probably thousands – of people like himself. And, like John Mack's Catherine, he gradually came to feel that these unpleasant experiences could be used positively, in the cause of personal evolution.

CONCLUSIONS

There can be no doubt that the researches conducted by Budd Hopkins, David Jacobs, John Mack and many others have thrown a completely new light on the UFO controversy. Their researches seem to suggest that the purpose of the 'space beings' is to somehow interbreed with the human race.

One UFO investigator, Donald Hotson, has suggested an interesting theory that seems to be, at least, consistent with the facts. Hotson is fascinated by the fact that human beings appear to have two completely independent 'modes of knowing', which have sometimes been described as 'left brain' and 'right brain'. The left cerebral hemisphere of the brain deals with language, logic, and with 'coping' with our everyday lives. The right hemisphere, on the other hand, seems to be more concerned with insight, intuition, artistic creativity. It might be said, in general terms, that the left brain is a scientist and the right brain an artist.

One of the most interesting observations made by brain physiologists is that our everyday personalities live in the left brain, while the being who lives only a few centimetres away in the right hemisphere is, in effect, a total stranger.

This was demonstrated in so-called 'split brain' experiments. The left and right hemispheres of the brain are connected by a knot of nerves called the *corpus callosum*. Sometimes, the corpus callosum is severed in order to prevent epileptic attacks. It was then observed that the patients behaved, in effect, like two people.

This could most easily be seen in experiments with the eyes. For some reason, the left halves of our bodies are connected to the right brain and the right halves of our bodies to the left brain. No one is quite certain why this should be so. It may also be said (in crude terms) that the right eye is connected to the left brain while the left eye is connected to the right brain.

If a split brain patient is shown an apple with the right eye and an orange with the left, (so that one eye cannot see what the other is seeing) and then asked what he has just seen, he will reply 'orange.' If asked to write with the left hand what he has just seen, he will write 'apple.' If asked what he has just written – without being allowed to look at it – he will reply 'orange.'

A split brain patient who was shown a pornographic picture with the right brain blushed. When asked why she was blushing she replied truthfully: 'I don't know.'

All this seems to demonstrate that the 'I' lives in the left brain, while an unknown self – which is also far more intuitive and creative than the 'I' – lives in the right brain.

There can be no possible doubt that civilisation has turned man increasingly into a 'left brain being'. It is necessary for his survival to develop a powerful sense of reason and logic, and to strengthen his ability to 'cope'. But the result is a partial repression of the intuitive self in the right brain. In moods of great happiness and relaxation, he may feel oddly 'unified', as if he has suddenly become aware of these intuitive reaches of his being.

It has also been frequently observed that primitive peoples seem to possess far more powerful intuitive faculties than their 'civilised' counterparts, and that many of them possess highly developed 'psychic' faculties.

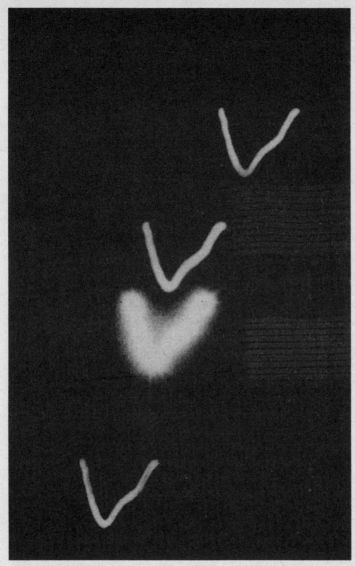

Four strange lights in the sky captured on film by a Columbus
Evening Dispatch photographer in Columbus, Ohio

Hotson asks, in effect, what would have happened if, at some remote period in time, the human race had virtually split into two types, one becoming increasingly logical and 'left brain', and the other increasingly intuitive and 'right brain'.

The historical answer would appear to be that this is, in fact, what has happened. Many human beings belong to the scientific and logical type, while others belong to the artistic and intuitive type.

But it is not entirely true to say that these two types are really different varieties of humanity. Even the most 'other worldly' artists speak the same language as the rest of us, and have to learn to cope with the practical world. In other words, they have been forced into the same accelerated left brain development as the most sceptical scientist or the most dogmatic Marxist.

But supposing, asks Hotson, the original 'right brainers' had preferred to pursue their own intuitive line of development? The first thing that would have happened is that the 'left brainers' would certainly have developed a basic hostility towards creatures they felt to be 'weirdos'. And the right brainers would have felt that the left brainers were stupid and short sighted materialists.

What if the right brainers finally decided that, in order to survive and pursue their own development, it would be necessary to withdraw entirely from the physical and material world?

This, then, is the suggestion thrown off by Hotson. The 'aliens' are highly developed right brainers, with whom we share a common origin. But we no longer share a common reality. As John Mack puts it: '[abductees] speak of aliens breaking through from another dimension, through a "slit" or "crack" in some sort of barrier, entering our world from "beyond the veil."'

But would such beings from 'beyond the veil' be able to reproduce? Would they not need the help of material humanity to prevent their own species from becoming completely static? This, Hotson suggests, could be the motive behind the 'hybrid programme'.

It is a fascinating hypothesis. Yet it has to be admitted that no hypothesis so far has succeeded in covering the extraordinary and complicated range of phenomena described by contactees. Why were the aliens who abducted Betty and Barney Hill round-faced and red-haired, so completely unlike the aliens described by Whitley Streiber and others? Who were the 'men in black' who visited so many contactees and warned them not to speak about what they had seen?

Whitley Strieber himself displayed an apparent change of heart in the introduction he wrote to a book called *The Omega Project* by Kenneth Ring. Ring originally became known as an investigator of so-called 'near death experiences', like those described in Raymond Moody's famous book *Life After Life* (1975). Moody had observed that a surprising number of patients who had been close to death had had the same experience of passing through a kind of tunnel towards a light, and had felt a marvellous sense of relief and happiness. In books like *Heading Towards Omega* and *Life at Death*, Ring had continued this study into the near death experience.

In *The Omega Project*, Ring points out certain similarities between the near death experience (NDE) and the abductee experience. And in his introduction, Strieber writes: 'This is not a book by a scientist who has somehow been seduced into believing in aliens. Indeed, this foreword has not been written by an author who has claimed "alien abduction". What I have claimed, and what Doctor Ring's study has found, is that the perceptions that are popularly referred to as "alien abduction" have some readily identifiable and highly unusual after effects in the lives of the people reporting them. This means that, like the near-death experience, the apparent alien encounter represents extremely powerful psychological material.'

He goes on: 'During the five years I struggled both with the experience and with a great deal of worldwide media attention, I learned the power of cultural conditioning. Despite the fact that I declared myself on behalf of keeping the question of the origin of the experience open time and time again, I was nevertheless introduced on my last major national television appearance as "self-proclaimed alien abductee Whitley Strieber". And despite the fact that the probable origin of the appearance of the phenomenon in the mind is the central theme of both my books on the subject, I have been more or less ostracized as a heretic from both the intellectual and literary communities.'

He later suggests: 'I would not, however, dismiss out of hand the seemingly fantastic notion that actual aliens may have their origin inside the human mind. After all, is not the Garden of the Gods inside us also? Even Christ acknowledged this when he located the Kingdom of Heaven within.

'Could it be that life itself is a mechanism by which some hidden, inner reality is touching and feeling its way into the physical world? Are we a medium of exchange, a communications device, an extraordinary construction designed to bridge the gulf between the physical world and something else?'

What Strieber seems to be suggesting is that the abductors are 'real', but not in the physical and material sense. They may be 'creatures from inner space'. *Not* creatures of imagination, but of some psychic depth where they exist like the creatures in the deepest parts of the ocean.

In *The Omega Project*, Ring develops the idea that the UFO experience should be classified with ghosts, poltergeists and religious visions. Most people who have experi-

enced NDEs have felt as though they had experienced some
higher form of reality. This often transformed their lives.
The same thing has happened with many people who have
had UFO experiences. Could there, Ring asks, be some
connection between the two?

After discussing many examples of NDEs and UFO
experiences, Ring proposes a bold theory. Our world is
haunted by fear of atomic catastrophe and the destruction of the environment. Is it not conceivable that both
NDEs and UFO experiences are some kind of response of
the 'collective unconscious' towards these fears? In other
words that they are some kind of hallucination — but a
hallucination from the depth of the collective unconscious, whose purpose is to force the human race to
evolve towards a higher level — a level at which it can
cope with these problems instead of being overwhelmed
by them?

Anyone who has read this book will have noticed how
the UFO phenomenon has changed subtly over the
years. At first, UFOs were believed (by those who
accepted their reality) to be simply craft from some
other planet or galaxy. Then, as increasing numbers
began to report 'missing time', it became clear that the
'aliens' appeared to have some powers that would
normally be labelled 'psychic'. In fact, the 'aliens' seem
to behave like the angels or the demons or ghosts which
our ancestors took for granted.

I have already pointed out that, in the mid-nineteenth
century, the sudden surge of interest in 'spiritualism' and life
after death led to the creation of the Society for Psychical
Research, and to the hope that, within the next few decades,
these things would be understood as confidently as the
phenomena of electricity or magnetism. In fact, every
attempt to create a comprehensive theory of the 'paranormal' ran into unforseen obstacles. When the Society for
Psychical Research had its centenary in 1982, it was clear

Photo of a flying saucer taken by George Adamski

that the whole subject was still as controversial as it had been in the mid-nineteenth century. Some members of the Society did not even believe in life after death.

What is now happening is that, as paranormal research spreads to every country in the world, and hundreds of cases are observed and recorded, scientists are beginning to apply the *statistical approach* to this huge mass of data. Since the development of 'chaos theory' in the 1980s, mathematicians are developing increasingly powerful tools for assessing the likelihood of some event. (It is sometimes called 'meta-analysis.') These tools demonstrate beyond all scientific doubt that parapsychology – the study of the paranormal – is studying real effects, not illusions. Now it is no longer a matter of sceptics thinking up a dozen reasons why every case *could* be a fraud. Mathematics itself, working on this immense body of data, has *proved* that a certain percentage of cases *must* be genuine.

To suggest that UFOs are basically 'psychic phenomena' may be to put it too crudely. It might be simply to say that the UFO phenomenon is the latest expression of something that has been happening down the centuries.

No one who has studied psychic phenomena can fail to observe that they seem to *change* over long periods of time.

Consider, for example, the strange history of the poltergeist, or 'banging ghost'. The earliest account we possess dates back to 858 AD in Germany, when an 'evil spirit' threw stones and shook the walls of a farmhouse 'as though men were striking them with hammers'. There are several other accounts over the next few centuries, but one thing is clear: that such cases were rare. Chroniclers are anxious to mention them as proof of the existence of the spirit world, and therefore of Christianity. If there had been many such cases, we should have heard about them.

Yet when I came to write a book about the poltergeist, I realised, to my astonishment, that there are literally hundreds of cases occurring all the time. In fact, it would probably be accurate to say that there is a poltergeist case taking place within ten miles of where you are at present reading this book. In other words, their *number* has increased dramatically.

Again, ghosts and 'spirits' were often recorded in earlier centuries. But in the mid-nineteenth century, when interest in 'spiritualism' swept the world from America to Russia, there were suddenly thousands of cases. It was as if the 'spirits' (or whatever they were) took advantage of this sudden interest in them to flood the world with their activities.

Perhaps the strangest case is that of the so-called vampire. Stories of vampires first reached the west in the early eighteenth century, when the Turks were driven out of eastern Europe. Doctors, priests and medical men reported cases in which dead people were seen walking the streets. When their graves were opened, their bodies were found undecayed, as if newly buried. Dozens of reliable witnesses signed sworn statements describing the exhumation of these 'living dead'. In fact, vampire stories date back many centuries, but in earlier times they often sound like poltergeists, creating disturbances rather than attacking living people. It is very difficult to pin down the truth behind the tales of the vampire. All we know is that it has *changed* down the centuries.

And now, suddenly, it seems that we have a new form of 'strange phenomenon', the UFO, complete with abductions and sinister men in black. Just as in the case of psychic phenomena, all efforts to understand it scientifically have run into a brick wall.

My own suggestion is that UFOs *are* some form of psychic phenomenon. They are not hallucinations, as Jung thought, neither are they genuine men from Mars. But it would be a mistake to say: in that case, they must be ghosts or poltergeists.

There is, I would suggest, another possibility, based upon the notion that there is a 'psychic reality' which runs *parallel* to our physical reality. Ghosts, demons, poltergeists, fairies, even 'vampires', are incursions from this 'other reality' into our own. Like the human race, the denizens of this other realm probably change and evolve, so their methods of drawing attention to themselves also change and evolve. In ancient times, there were simply ghosts, believed to be spirits of the dead. In the Middle Ages came poltergeists. In the 17th century there were vampires. In the 19th century, there were all kinds of 'spirit communicators'.

In the second half of the 20th century there are UFOs. In the 21st century, there will probably be some new wave of 'strange phenomena' which at present we cannot even imagine.

Do these phenomena have a 'purpose?' That is impossible to say; but one thing is very clear: that their *effect* is to remind human beings that their material world is not the only reality. We are surrounded by mystery that *cannot* be understood in terms of scientific materialism. If psychic phenomena have a purpose it is to wake us up from our 'dogmatic slumber', and galvanise us to evolve a higher form of consciousness. I would suggest that this is the only positive and unambiguous lesson we can learn from the strange mystery of the flying saucers.

Titles in the World Famous series

World Famous Cults and Fanatics

World Famous Scandals

World Famous Strange Tales and Weird Mysteries

World Famous Crimes of Passion

World Famous Unsolved Crimes

World Famous Catastrophes

World Famous Strange but True

World Famous True Ghost Stories

World Famous Gangsters

World Famous Robberies

World Famous Weird News Stories

World Famous SAS and Elite Forces

World Famous Royal Scandals

World Famous UFOs

World Famous Unsolved

World Famous War Heroes

World Famous True Love Stories

World Famous Spies